PACHAMAMA

Our Earth - Our Future

By young people of the world

A joint project of the
United Nations Environment Programme and Peace Child International

Evans Brothers Ltd

© 1999 United Nations Environment Programme, P O Box 30552, Nairobi, Kenya
Phone: +254 2 62 12 34; website: http://www.unep.org
Published for and on behalf of UNEP by Evans Brothers Limited
2A Portman Mansions, Chiltern Street, London W1M 1LE, UK

Project Coordinator: David Woollcombe
Layout, design and cover illustration: Cecilia Weckström
Project Administrators: Christine Jasinski, Urjana Shrestha, Hanna Rådberg
Editor for Evans Brothers Limited: Su Swallow
Project Supervision at UNEP: Marion Cheatle
UNEP Project Consultant: Jennifer Castleden

Experts Advisory Group:
Noel J. Brown, Marion Cheatle, Edgar E. Gutiérrez-Espeleta, Julia Heiss, Khalid Irani,
Theodore Oben, Elizabeth Odera, Mamata Pandya, Jingjing Qian, Veerle Vandeweerd.

Educational Advisory Group:
David Batten, Anne Clarke, Julian Cottendon, Isabelle Donaday, Tom Jolly

With thanks to UNICEF and UNESCO for their support of this project

*Peace Child International wishes to extend a special thanks to Veerle Vandeweerd for dreaming up
this wonderful project, and providing us with support and expertise on all issues
related to the global environment.*

The production of this book was made possible by a grant from the
United Nations Fund for International Partnerships

Printed in Hong Kong by Wing King Tong Co. Ltd. on chlorine-free paper from
sustainably managed forests

British Library Cataloguing in Publication Data
Pachamama: our earth, our future
1. Environmental protection – Juvenile literature
333.1
ISBN: 0 237 52119 9
Much of the material in this book is derived from the UNEP GEO-2000 Report [ISBN: 1 853 83588 9]
published by Earthscan Publications Ltd, London, UK

The CD-ROM (PC&Mac) to accompany Pachamama will be
available from April 2000. For your discount copy, write to Peace Child
International (address shown below) enclosing a cheque, eurocheque or credit
card authorisation for £ 3.95/$ 6.50 incl. postage and packaging.

Peace Child International, The White House International Centre, Buntingford,
Herts. SG9 9AH, UK, +44 (0) 176 327 4459, www.peacechild.org

PACHAMAMA

Our Earth - Our Future

Editors:

Mohammed Al-Abbas (Jordan), Melina D'Auria (Argentina), Viola Caretti (Italy),
Claude Didace (Benin), Cecilia Farfan (Mexico), Dominique Mansilla Hermann (Argentina),
Marina Mansilla Hermann (Argentina), Andrew Hobbs (Australia), Ikramah Jafar (Seychelles),
Steven Appollo Kalule (Uganda), Michelle Luxon (Canada), Mossi Frances Oloo (Kenya),
Ali Abbas Panju (Kenya), Astri Rahayu (Indonesia), Martina Rizza (Italy), Benedetta Rossi (Italy),
Renée Royal (Alaska, USA), Hassan Al Saleh (Oman), Hajara Kader Sani (Niger),
Céline Schwob (France), Srijana Shrestha (Nepal), Neha Smriti (India), Pili Vicente (Spain)

Fore*word*

Young people from all over the world have produced an inspiring, sometimes frightening, collection of case studies, poems and drawings to tell the story of our global environment. Some things they have to say are disturbing – adults have acted irresponsibly in caring for the environment. But young people are also enthusiastically dedicated to their future – a future where Mother Earth is healthy and where people work together to solve our current and future problems.

Over a year ago, when this book was still only an idea, Brem, a young Indian man said:

'By creating this book, young people world-wide can work together and produce something really amazing. Once we know what the problems look like in each part of the world, we will have a much better idea of what we each have to do to solve them.'

How right he was.

As you read, *Pachamama* will tell you why the world's environment is being degraded and how our Mother Earth is doing today. The book also tells you about what is being done around the world and maybe even on your doorstep, to protect the environment. And, as we move into the next century and millennium, the book looks at what we can expect in the future. It ends with a set of true stories relating what young people around the world are doing to improve their environment. I hope you will enjoy reading *Pachamama* and become inspired to take action.

A lot of information in *Pachamama* has come out of a book called the Global Environment Outlook, or GEO in short. GEO is a report written by the United Nations Environment Programme (UNEP). The report is an overview of the

The partners acknowledge the following UNEP staff and others who reviewed the draft of Pachamama

UNEP: Mahmood Y. Abdulraheem; Yinka Adebayo; Wondwosen Asnake; Karine Bachmann; Barbara Bierhuizen; Ulf Carlsson; Jennifer Castleden; Marion Cheatle; Gerry Cunningham; Arthur Dahl; Salif Diop; Norberto Fernandez; Abdullah Hadi; Beth Ingraham; Bob Kakuyo; Donald Kaniaru; Christian Lambrechts; Theodore Oben; Ayub A.A. Osman; Naomi Poulton; Vijay Samnotra; Ricardo Sanchez; Jim Sniffen; Chantravadee Songkran; Cheikh Sow; Anna Stabrawa; Mick Wilson; Ronald G. Witt; Kaveh Zahedi; Jinhua Zhang

GEO-for-Youth Partner Organisations and Advisors: Gustavo Lopez Ospina, UNESCO; Jingjing Qian, UNICEF; Mamata Pandya, Centre for Environmental Education, India

health or state of our environment and of the policies that are in place to manage the environment and tackle environmental problems.

To produce this report, UNEP works with hundreds of people and many organisations around the world, who collect and send us information about the environment and what people are doing about it. UNEP compiles all this information into the GEO report. *Pachamama* was made in a similar way. Young people from all over the world wrote to UNEP, and UNEP's partner Peace Child International, about the environment in their country. From all the contributions, an editorial group made up of some of the authors and artists compiled the stories, poems, case studies and pictures into this amazing book.

When you have finished reading *Pachamama*, I challenge you to do the following:

1. Talk about the problems that you see in your own environment with your friends, family and teachers.

2. Make an action plan on how you can improve your environment in the new millennium – and write to me in twelve months telling me the difference that you have made.

3. Challenge yourself and your leaders to bring the concept of sustainable development, especially environmental and social justice, to the centre of local, national and international decision-making.

It's your world -
accept nothing less.

Dr. Klaus Töpfer
Executive Director
United Nations Environment Programme

GEO Collaborating Centres: Jan Bakkes, National Institute of Public Health and the Environment, Netherlands; Seema Deo, South Pacific Regional Environment Programme, Samoa; Edgar Gutiérrez-Espeleta, University of Costa Rica; Yateendra Joshi, Tata Energy Research Institute, India; Leena Srivastava, Tata Energy Research Institute, India; Osvaldo Sunkel, Sustainable Development Program, University of Chile; Le Anh Tuan, Asian Institute of Technology, Thailand

UNEP Youth Advisory Council: Anthony Ambahan, Philippines; Vinothini Apok, Singapore; Luis Betanzos, Mexico; Amexo Dickson, Ghana; Tsvetvan Ivanov, Bulgaria; Aditi Jindal, India; Sharon Makoriwa, Kenya; Ngue Awane Michel, Burkina Faso; Doug Ragan, Canada; Celine Schwob, France; Tamoifo Nkkom Marie, Cameroon; Vipada Ungvichian, Thailand; Adriana Zacharias, Mexico

CONTENTS

60-75

76-91

Our Future

What We Can Do!

92-96

Ecomind Maze

PACHAMAMA
Our Earth – Our Future

Introduction

It's after midnight and loud salsa music is playing. The Latin American gang is trying to get everyone to party. A few are asleep, but most of us are either raiding the fridge for snacks or chatting, enjoying each other's company!

Welcome to a typical moment in the lives of the *Pachamama* editors. You must be wondering why we chose a name like *Pachamama* for our book. Well, one young person told us, 'I have visited South America and I have a personal relationship with *Pachamama*. I know her – she exists. She breathes in the forests, she rages in the earthquakes and the volcanoes, she flows through the rivers and crashes on the shore with the sea. I feel her arms around me, nurturing me and all she asks of me in return is to love her, care for her, nurture her.'

That is what this book is about: each one of us learning to establish a personal relationship with our Mother, the Earth and caring for her in the same way that we do for our friends and family.

The original Global Environment Outlook Report (GEO-2000) was prepared by the United Nations Environment Programme (UNEP) with environmental institutions around the world. It does not shrink from telling us how bad some things are, and how they could get much, much worse during our lifetimes. But it also tells us how much good is happening. We are turning the corner – but the trouble is we are not turning it fast enough. That is why young people are so important to the movement – we have to get in there and energise adults with our ideas and action so that we do change our habits and save Mother Earth for our children and grandchildren.

Producing this book has been an amazing process. First, hundreds of groups around the world were recruited to read and summarise the chapters of the original GEO. These contributors came up with some wonderful stories, paintings and ideas. The hardest thing was deciding which to include, for we could have made 10 books! The book you have

A guide to graphic devices:

in your hands was put together by two editorial teams and a group of adult experts who came from around the world to give us their advice on the first draft. The final text was checked by UNEP.

The editors represent all the different regions of our world, speak different languages and have very different backgrounds. We had never met before and yet we quickly became a happy team. We argued, brainstormed and pushed ourselves and each other to make this the best possible book on the environment there is.

The only measure of our success that we care about is that, when you get to the end of this book, you will be inspired to leap up and do something to save our precious Mother Earth. For what we learned from each other and all the inspiring contributions by the young people is that we are all responsible – in everything we do, every day of our lives. So start TODAY. Listen to *Pachamama*'s urgent message: she is our shelter... she is LIFE.

Key information drawn from the UNEP Global Environment Outlook Report

Case study / contribution from a young person

International United Nations convention / agreement

Contribution by the Editors

WHAT DO YOU THINK? Some key issues for you to discuss

See the CD-ROM for more information / case studies / interviews [available April 2000 - see page 2]

Welcome *on board...*

"Ladies and gentlemen! This is your information officer speaking to you from the GEO Information Centre of Spaceship Planet Earth. As you know, there are no passengers on this spaceship. We are all, in a sense, pilots."

"We all have an impact on our route and flight plan. This update is just to tell you that, from here, it looks like you're all making a pretty poor job of it! I would like to wish you all a pleasant life-flight, but I've just checked out the computer projections and I have to tell you that, if you behave as recklessly as your parents, the good ship Planet Earth will crash sometime in the not too distant future!

This need not happen, of course, but all of you out there, especially those of you who are chewing up its surface and wasting its fuel, will have to choose a different flight plan – and do it pretty soon if this flight is going to have a happy ending. Thank you and choose your flight plan carefully."

" If people suddenly disappeared from the Earth, the planet could recover and, within 1,000 years, it would look as it did 100,000 years ago. If insects disappeared, nothing on land would survive. **"**
Rafael Gonzalez Urdaneta, Mexico

Idir Kerkovehe, Algeria

GEO'S Message

That flight report, in brief, is the message of GEO. There are many signs that we are waking up to the need for a change of attitudes and practices towards the environment, but the sad truth is, it is not happening nearly fast enough! GEO defines three driving forces affecting our global environment – political and economic problems made worse by rapid population growth. Without the social, economic and political problems caused by humans, the global environment would probably be in much better shape.

The Facts

Experts continuously improve ways to measure the state of our environment – and things like population growth that affect it. But the information does not get out to most of you. You get regular reports on the weather and stock markets, but you rarely hear news of world grain yields or species extinction rates. GEO fills this gap by bringing us the latest news, issue by issue. These issues are explored in the Our Earth section (pages 14 - 59). Our Future (pages 60 - 77) explains what governments, other groups and individuals are doing about these issues.

POPULATION GROWTH

One of the hardest things is to ensure a sustainable life for the six billion people on the Earth, and the 78 million who join us every year. If we can control birth rates, scientists predict that our numbers will reach about nine billion by 2050. However, unchecked, world population could rise to 27 billion! At present consumption rates, this would put our world's resources under enormous pressure.

ECONOMY

The richest countries of the world, called "developed countries", have 20% of the world's population but they use 60% of the world's energy resources. Economics are driven by the choices people make and the values they hold. To decrease consumption, we will have to change our behaviour and our belief that more is better.

Good News

Some of the international agreements, like the Montreal Protocol (to stop the hole in the ozone layer from widening) and the Convention on International Trade in Endangered Species of Flora and Fauna (CITES) are really working, and some environmental problems are receding. But we have to move faster, invest in saving the environment and create new institutions to work on it!

POLitics

The political power of national governments is decreasing. This is a result of globalisation. Countries are dominated by what is best for trade and the pursuit of money, not what is best for communities and the environment. GEO-2000 suggests we need a new approach to governance that will protect the Earth and its inhabitants. In all countries, 20 to 45% of national income is given by citizens to central government for security and state services. The United Nations is given practically nothing to provide those services globally. A global tax on tourism or currency exchange would raise money to help save our environment and ensure only those who can afford to pay are taxed.

Education Gap

Education is vital. Those of us who know what is happening to the world around us are determined to do something about it. Knowledge is power and the six billion pilots of this spaceship need that knowledge NOW! That is the purpose of GEO. It is why we wrote this book. So – enjoy it! Use it! Act upon it!

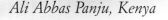

Ali Abbas Panju, Kenya

Imagine approaching our Earth from space. You float down through the atmosphere and encounter freshwater in the form of rain. Because 70% of our planet's surface is sea water, you probably land on the sea. You are washed up on the shore, and you encounter land. Moving inland, you find the forests where you discover biodiversity – the variety of plants and animals. Further on, you come to cities! Finally, you move to the planet's extremes and reach the polar regions. Welcome to the richness of Our Earth's environment!

Our Earth

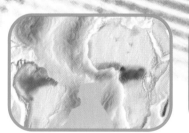

ℹ Atmosphere

Until the Earth's protective atmosphere was formed, there was no life except in the sea. Now big cities, cars and factories pollute the air so much, we may soon be better off back there! GEO-2000 tells us there has been some improvement, but it is not fast enough.

Air Pollution

Our planet is becoming choked with poisonous gases mostly from our daily activities like driving cars, warming our houses and running power stations. The problem is worst in Latin America and Asia. In cities like Seoul and Mexico City, the air is so bad, some people wear face masks to filter the air they breathe. In cities like Beirut and Damascus, dust storms make it even worse! And pollution doesn't need a passport. Pollution from factories and power stations in Europe, North America and Russia ends up in the Arctic region.

Human Health

Air pollution is a major factor in causing humans to get ill. Tuberculosis, bronchitis, heart and chest diseases, stomach disorders, asthma and cancers can all be traced to chemicals in the air. Pesticides and fertilisers release gases and particles into the air which poison people and kill animals.

Ali Abbas Panju, Kenya, based on an idea by Noelia V. Cocco, Argen

Imagine that the Earth has a sunshade around it protecting it from the heat of the sun. This is called the ozone layer but the sunshade has holes so that harmful rays get through, causing cancer. To prevent it, we wear sun glasses to protect our eyes, and sun cream to protect our skin. *Ling So Low, Malaysia*

Ozone depletion

For years, chlorofluorocarbons (CFCs) were used as a cooling device in freezers and air conditioners. Scientists discovered, however, that CFCs destroy the ozone layer – the layer that filters ultraviolet radiation from the sun. Ultraviolet radiation causes eye damage and skin cancer. An international agreement commonly called the Montreal Protocol, signed in 1989 (see page 62), has helped stop the production of CFCs. If we keep to this agreement, ozone-depleting substances will stop being produced and the ozone layer will begin to repair itself over the next 100 years.

Global Warming

The world is warming up because carbon dioxide (CO_2) from smoke and car exhausts collects in the atmosphere and traps some of the heat going back to space, like a greenhouse. CO_2 and other greenhouse gases are expected to raise global temperature by an average of 2°C by the year 2100 causing the polar icecaps to melt, sea levels to rise and freak weather conditions which may cause millions of deaths.

Death *in the air*

In most places, we have to wash our windows regularly. Why? Because they get clogged with pollution from the air. But that is the same air we breathe – and we can't wash our lungs. Sometimes, the dirt in the air can kill us.

Dirty Brown Air

When the clouds get so dirty and brown,
It is not a nice thing: it makes us all frown!
All the cars and buses put smoke in the air
Don't they know that it's not really fair?
All the rubbish that people throw on the ground
After a few years will become a big mound –
A mound that gives out the most terrible smell
Which is what makes this planet a living hell.

Instead of this hell that we're all living in
Let's now work together to make sure we all win!
Instead of a car, why not buy a bike?
And instead of a drive, why not take a hike?
From now on, don't you dare ever litter the floor
Just try to remember you'd be breaking the law.
Forget throwing waste away – just recycle, re-use!
Then share with your friends the good news!

Arouge Chaudhry, Tajmnia Chaudhey, Aimee Rebdon
and Debi Moncur, England, UK

CHEMICAL FATALITY

The accident at the Union Carbide factory in Bhopal, India was one of the worst industrial disasters in history. One December night in 1984, a Union Carbide worker noticed gas escaping from a 70,000 litre tank of methyl isocyanate – a deadly gas. As it escaped into the atmosphere, it caused the almost instant death of 2,500 people. Another 350,000 became very sick with breathing problems and stomach aches – some of which continue to this day!

The accident was bad enough. What happened afterwards was almost worse: Union Carbide has never admitted responsibility for the disaster and has not apologised to its victims. They have paid minimal compensation to those who lost loved ones and have done little to provide medical care to the 50,000 or so who still suffer and cannot earn as much as they might have done had they not been injured in the accident. Government needs to be tougher on companies like Union Carbide. When charged with homicide, the company did not bother to appear at the court, only appearing when the charges were reduced to negligence.

Neha Smriti, India

"If I were Head of State, I would control enterprises and make sure they obeyed environmental laws strictly. I would punish them severely if they broke the laws."
Boris Medvedev, Ukraine

Avohpo, Benin

Smog *in the mind*

Smog is thick, choking, dangerous. It happens when tiny particles of dust, smoke and dangerous gases like sulphur dioxide mix with water vapour. And it's no accident: it is all carefully manufactured by one species – human beings!

The Furnacite Plant

The Furnacite Plant
When it was there
Polluted our air.
Now that it's gone,
The legacy lives on.

Underground
Out of sight,
Lurks toxic waste
Another blight
The legacy lives on.

Cara Meade, Wales, UK

Mad Car Disease

Today, cars are becoming like a disease. They are spreading so fast: 100,000 new cars are leaving factories every day. There are 400 million cars on the road. A bus can carry 60 people and doesn't give off as many fumes as 60 cars.

Aimee Robson, England, UK

Smog in the city

Smog is something we live through almost every day in Mexico City. Most mornings you wake up with red eyes; coughing and being sick is pretty common too.

Clean days are rare compared to those where you can see the smog produced by cars and factories hanging over the hillsides, curling down the freeways, wrapping its arms around the tall buildings. The government has tried to reduce the smog, but it hasn't worked. Citizens still get sick and children are the most affected. Red eyes, skin covered with a layer of grime, a knotted feeling of sick in your stomach – that's how you feel most days in the world's biggest city.

Cecilia Farfan, Mexico

Not My Fault!

It is Friday. As usual, I get up at 7 am and on my way to the bathroom I turn on the coffee machine. I take the milk out of the fridge. I take a long shower and finish with a quick squirt from a spray deodorant. After breakfast I run to the car and fight the traffic for half an hour to get to the office.

It looks like a nice sunny day but I have to spend it in our air-conditionned office. For lunch, I order packaged food from a catering service: hamburgers and french fries (they stay nice and warm in the foam plastic cartons). To finish up there's hot coffee in a foam cup. My afternoon is filled with meetings and a few long phone calls.

Tired, I get back into the car and drive home. On my way I pick up my suits from the dry cleaners. Once home, I sit down in my favourite armchair and watch a TV programme on the greenhouse effects. The situation seems very bad. They really should do something about it. Nothing to do with me, of course! – Or is it?

Anonymous

Marisol Garcia Ochoa, Mexico

People love cars, most of us want one! What can we do to end this love affair with the car before it ends us?
*Alfred Kamara,
Sierra Leone*

Uneven distribution

Some areas have far too much water and suffer from floods, like Bangladesh and the flood plains of the Mississippi in the United States. Other areas, like Africa and West Asia, suffer severe droughts. The problem of water availability is most serious in Africa and West Asia. If water consumption continues at its present rate, by 2025 two out of three people will not have enough water for their basic needs.

Pollution

Mining and industry pollute rivers with deadly chemicals. Farmers spray crops with pesticides and fertilisers which are washed into rivers and lakes. In many parts of the world, people use rivers as open sewers and garbage dumps. Near coasts, when too much water is taken from aquifers (big underground reservoirs of fresh water), sea water seeps in and makes the water salty and undrinkable.

Depleting resources

If you take more money out of a bank than you put in, you get an overdraft and eventually go broke. We are doing this to our aquifers all over the world. In West Asia, North Africa, China, India, Russia and the USA, we run huge annual water overdrafts. This, combined with the discharge of untreated industrial waste and sewage into water systems makes water shortage one of our most critical environmental issues.

Human Health

Worldwide, polluted water affects the health of 1.2 billion people and contributes to the death of 15 million children under five every year. For example, in Asia, one in three people do not have access to safe drinking water and one in two have no access to hygienic sanitation.

Picture facing page: Kevin Day, Jamaica

"
Though everything may
seem everlasting,
caring should start from
the youth in me.
"

Angela Shima, Philippines

Water *pollution*

If you had a bottle of life-preserving fluid on which your life depended, would you pour into it all your sewage and rubbish, along with any other poisonous chemicals you could find? And yet, that is exactly what we are doing to our water supply – all over the world.

Riverbend

Zukas and Cosmo lived in a small village, by a small river. The village didn't have any running water and so they had to go to fetch water every day at the river. Cosmo liked working and cared about his health. Zukas on the other hand was lazy and careless about his health. One day, Zukas was sent to fetch some water. He met Cosmo on the way. "Hi Zukas! Going to Rapid Point?" "No, Riverbend. Rapid Point is just too far."

"But the water is not safe there!" said Cosmo. Zukas took no notice. On the way back from Riverbend, he fell asleep under a tree and dreamed mosquitoes as big as cars were chasing him. He jumped into the river and saw snails as big as buildings and huge, ugly germs and insects. They all chased him and he started shouting for help. He woke up and immediately threw away his water and ran to Rapid Point. He never fetched water from Riverbend again. But he still likes dodging work. It's still the same old Zukas, just a bit wiser...

Loveness Chisha, Zambia

BroWN Water

Since February 1998, the residents of Adamawa State in Nigeria have been experiencing brown water running out of their taps. This is a common problem in many developing countries. It has led to the outbreak of cerebral meningitis and hookworm. Up until the time of this publication, the residents of Yola have been particularly badly affected.

Daniel Onyi Eboh, Nigeria.

GaNga'S SickNeSS

According to Hindu beliefs, the Goddess Ganga descended to Earth in the form of a river in order to purify the souls of 60,000 dead princes. The River Ganges symbolises purification for millions of Hindus around the world, and many make their way to it, believing that drinking the waters will give them salvation.

Today there are 400 million people living along the banks of the river in 29 cities, 70 towns and hundreds of villages. These people deposit nearly all their sewage – almost 1.3 billion litres per day – directly into the river.

Add to this the 260 million litres of industrial waste from the many factories along the river. This – like the sewage – enters the river mostly untreated. Also, there is the runoff from more than six million tons of chemical fertilisers and pesticides sprayed on the fields along its length. Thus, this holy symbol of purification has become an open sewer of shame to its people.

Neha Smriti, India

Luis Vargas, Mexico

Ext*remes*

It's crazy, isn't it? There are millions of people in deserts, desperate for a drop of water, while millions of others fight back the flood water, desperate for the rain to stop.

Too Little

"It was one of the worst years my parents could remember. Each day, I had to walk 20 kilometres to find a well to fill my bucket. The walk back was the worst – the bucket was so heavy on my head that I swear my neck had shrunk by the time I got home. One day, the well dried up and I had to look for water in the ponds. My mum had to boil it to get rid of the dirt and microbes. This takes ages and you have to wait until it cools down before you can use it. But it's OK. It's what you have to do if you live in a dry, hot country."

Hajara Kader, Niger

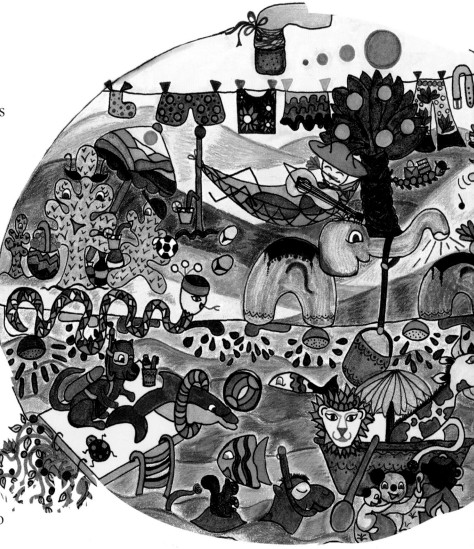

Viola Caretti, Italy

TOO MUCH

The rains started in October, 1997 and ended in mid-April, 1998: six months of disaster in Kenya. People and animals drowned, crops were flooded, and bridges and roads were spoiled by the deluge of water. Even today, many of the roads have not been repaired in the poorer areas of the country. Waterborne diseases such as cholera, dysentery, typhoid and bilharzia increased due to the rains. In a developing country such as Kenya, people have a hard time finding the money to rebuild their homes. Where crops and farms were destroyed, others also lost their jobs. With global warming, the floods will only get worse.

Julie Nailantei, Kenya

FLOODS IN PERU

Ica is a city situated on the banks of a river that flows west from the Andes to the Pacific across the arid, Ica desert. It very rarely rains. The extreme increase in rainfall in the Andes during the 1997-98 El Niño storms made the river flood. The houses in Ica are built of adobe (mud bricks) that simply get washed away when it rains too hard. During El Niño, half the city was washed away. Homes, schools, health clinics, places of work were devastated. It has set the city back years.

Tomás Julio, Peru

SQUEEZING OUR PLANET DRY

Water consumption has increased everywhere in the last 50 years. In Western Europe between 1950 and 1990, it grew from 100 to 560 cubic kilometres a year – after which it has declined a little. In Asia, it has increased from 600 to 5,000 cubic kilometres between 1900 and the mid-1980s. In Beijing, water consumption increased almost 100 times from 1950 to 1980. With limited amounts of water, unevenly distributed, these increases place great stress on our water supply. The crazy thing is that, even in developed countries, huge quantities of water are lost through leaky pipes. In parts of Central Asia, the pipes are so bad, over half the water is lost through leaks.

Look at the average water consumption per person in different parts of our world. The average North American is using more than eight times as much as an average African uses.

in cubic metres per person

World average	645
Africa	202
North America	1,798

ℹ Marine & *coastal areas*

Oceans are the largest ecosystems on Earth. Seventy-five per cent of all sea pollution is from land-based human activity. People abuse the coastal marine environment by destroying habitats, by over-fishing and pollution.

Crowded coasts

More than 37% of the world's population lives within 100 km of a coast and this percentage is rising! Land prices are rising too, forcing change in economic activity and forcing out local fishing villagers.

Sea Pollution

Most countries use the sea as a sewer. For example, coastal cities in Africa dump hundreds of millions of litres of sewage and industrial waste into the sea a year. This will continue as they cannot afford sewage treatment plants. As sewage, fertilisers and other 'nutrients' are poured into the seas, sea weeds and algae spread like a horror movie, using up all the oxygen that fish need to stay alive. In the past, the Soviets dumped nuclear waste in the shallow seas of the Arctic circle. As these began to leak, the marine life came under threat.

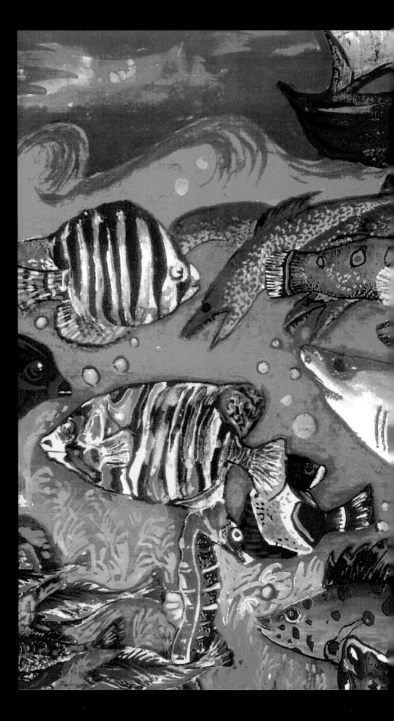

Over-Fishing

World fish catches peaked in 1987 and are now falling. Why? Because modern fishing techniques suck up *too many* fish, large and small so there are not enough young fish left to breed.

Mangroves

Coastal mangrove forests are major breeding grounds for many fish and crustaceans but they are being wiped out for housing and fish-farming. In Asia – home to 87% of the world's fish farms – huge areas of mangrove swamps have disappeared and along with them, the fish nurseries! Fish farms are dangerous in themselves because diseases spread from the farmed fish and affect the wild fish.

Coral Reefs

Coral reefs are like the rainforests of the sea, supporting many fish. But 60% of them are dying, mainly as a result of pollution from human activity. Dead coral reefs mean dead seas, no fish and fewer tourists who pay to visit the reefs!

Sea Mammals

Save the whales! This slogan made Greenpeace, an international environmental organisation, famous, and it still applies. Whales, dolphins and many big sea mammals have been hunted to the point of extinction. They need our protection.

Foundation for Global Peace and the Environment, Japan

Sea *of slaughter*

Oceans support life, drive our climate, provide our rainfall and are a vital source of food. Yet humans have devised new and deadly ways to slaughter the inhabitants of our seas, endangering the marine environment for all of us.

BLOWN AWAY!

Dynamite fishing involves explosives which kill every creature in the water. Young people reported this happening in Sri Lanka, the Philippines, Tanzania, Liberia and the Caribbean.

VANISHING ACt

Whales are the biggest animals in the world. Some are up to 30 metres long and weigh almost 35 tonnes. Whales are very important: they help conserve the balance of the ocean ecosystem. If you tamper with that balance, the whole ecosystem is threatened.

There are about 43 whale species world-wide, but some are under threat. Roughly 4500 individual whales come to the principal beaches in Mexico, but their numbers are decreasing. It's unfair the way people violate the international agreements and keep killing them. *Alejandro Elnecave, Mexico*

" Construction companies extract a lot of sand from the beaches. This brings the sea shore nearer to coastal civilisation. Because of this, the seas destroy a lot of coastal resorts and houses during high tide. *Claude Didace, Benin*

Velikanova Nataliya, Ukraine

Black Sea Grief

Over the last 30 years, catches of valuable fish in the Black Sea have declined to a twentieth of their former level. Shellfish harvests have dropped by a similar amount – all due to the fact that 400 cubic kilometres of human and industrial waste pour into the Black Sea every year, mostly via the rivers that flow into the sea from surrounding countries.

The problem of river pollution along great rivers like the Danube, the Dnieper and the Dniester all become one big problem when they reach the Black Sea.

Skorikova Zlata, Ukraine

Gentle Manatees

The manatees are in danger of extinction off the Florida coast. There are fewer than 1200 left and they are disappearing fast. A major cause is the tourist boats. The motors of the boats slash into the bodies of manatees which swim very near the surface.

Liliana Fonseca Real, USA

A Fishy Tragedy

The Grand Banks off Newfoundland were renowned for their abundance of cod fish. When European explorers first arrived, they heard rumours that there were so many fish in the sea, you could almost walk on the water. Today there are practically none. Sadly, fishing fleets took too many fish. The level of fishing was unsustainable. The legacy is unemployment and frustration in maritime Canada.

Michelle Luxon, Canada
picture courtesy of
Foundation for Global Peace and
Environment, Japan

My dying *blue universe*

I was almost home after a long, dangerous sea voyage.
Two days ago, my friend and I were chased by humans who
threw spears at us. My friend was killed, but I got away as
they pulled him into their boat. One of the spears had
pierced my flipper, an aching reminder of the loss of my
friend. Still, even in my pain, I had the urge to swim
quickly to reach my home.

A sinking feeling touched me as I reached my
birthing grounds – I saw the sad state of my
favourite coral reef. It had been the most
beautifully formed coral reef I had ever seen in
all my years of travel. Now colourless broken
corals were scattered everywhere. Cans and
rubbish were stuck in coral. The gardens of
my memory lay in ruins.

While studying these changes, I
didn't see what was ahead of
me – until it was too late. A
net! While struggling to get
free, I was violently pulled to
the surface. Humans hoisted
me out of the water and I was
hung from a hook and poked
with tools. Then the humans
did the strangest thing –
they put me back in the
water. My fear and exhaustion were almost overwhelming but I struggled on
painfully. Upon reaching the top of the beach, blood trailed behind me. I had
been cut by glass left in the sand.

picture by Velarde González, Mexico

Slowly I dug a deep hole. I laid my eggs, rested briefly and then headed for the sea. The lives of my babies might be difficult in the decaying seas of the world, but our species would carry on. I reached the water and waves of white foam washed over me. Feeling weak from blood loss, I suddenly felt as if I was choking. Something was covering my head. A plastic bag! I had no more energy to wriggle it off. As my pulse began to slow, my eyes closed into darkness.

On the beach, a heavy construction machine lifted the sand into a pickup truck to make way for Paradise, the newest tourist resort being developed in the area. Nobody noticed the turtle eggs in the sand.

Helena Sims, Seychelles

Land *and food*

Good soils and growing conditions are not evenly distributed around the world and in places the problem is made worse by a greedy few abusing the land, resulting in poverty and hunger for millions.

Land Degradation

Soil degradation affects a third of the world's land and diminishes our ability to produce food for the growing population. It is caused by deforestation, poor land and water management, over-use of fertilisers and pesticides, poor waste disposal, clearance of poor land for growing food, and air pollution. Land degradation leads in a helter-skelter downward spiral to worse poverty amongst the world's poorest peoples.

Desertification

Extreme land degradation results in desertification - when land becomes desert and is unable to support any vegetation. Desertification affects over a billion people. It is particularly bad in the savannas of Africa, the Great Plains and pampas of the Americas and in the steppes of south-east Europe and Asia, the outback of Australia and parts of the Mediterranean region.

> " Soil destruction in Bosnia-Herzegovina comes from war. Aggression has caused an immense wave of migration. The new settlements are built on prime agricultural land. Where will we grow our food now? "
>
> *Nerina Zagora, Bosnia*

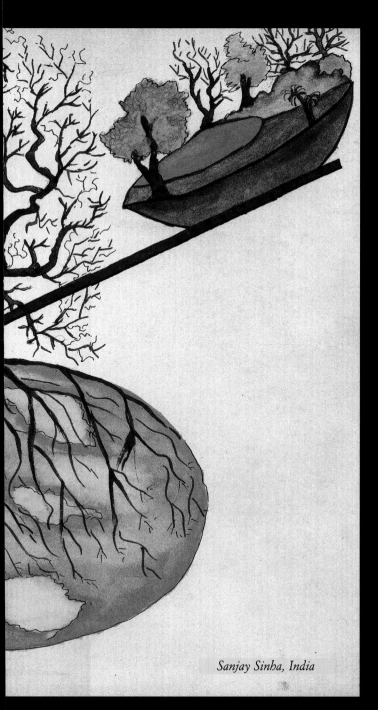

Sanjay Sinha, India

Rapid Urbanisation

Towns and cities are often developed on former farmland and forests. As urban areas grow, land that once grew food disappears under concrete. This means the remaining land has to produce more food to support even more people. Poverty increases stress, especially in Asia where 75% of the people are poor. Available land per capita is already very low in Asia with 182 people per km^2 compared to the world average of 44 per km^2.

Food Security

Food security is all about having enough food. Food availability in sub-Saharan Africa and Southeast Asia is a huge problem now. The countries in these regions generally have the fastest growing populations. They also have the largest number of poor people, the worst land degradation, most rapid urbanisation and biggest debts so they cannot afford to import food. GEO tells us that in the year 2000, 38 developing countries will have serious food security risks and be unable to feed even half their people from traditional farming practices.

Food – *glorious food!*

The main reason that people are concerned about the state of the land at the moment is for food. Some parts of the world can produce more food than they need, but many have far too little.

Hope in the Sahara

My home town of Keita is a small, farming community. Generally, there is enough food: our markets are full of vegetables, most of us manage to eat meat once a day and there is enough water most of the time. But life in the Sahara is hard. We live a simple life. People are not always happy – poverty makes finding food every day difficult. In times of drought, which is often caused by desertification, life gets very hard. But there is some hope. With help from international organisations, the Niger government has rescued 25,000 hectares from soil degradation. Sixteen million trees have been planted, 40 big dams and 235 little dams have been built to irrigate fields. Farmers have set up cooperatives, sharing resources and machinery, and learning techniques from each other. The young people in my town now have jobs to look forward to.

Hajara Kader, Niger

picture by Avohpo, Benin

⚠ Losing Quality Food

> ❓ "Everything has its limits. Do you know where those limits are? No? Neither do I – so is there any limit to the number of people our world can support? "
>
> *Olga Yakovleva, Russia*

India has an economy that is based on agriculture. It is a leading producer and exporter of rice in the world, giving us a lot of foreign exchange. But it is a pity that the people of India themselves cannot get good quality rice in their diet. In my view, the government should restrict the amount of rice exported and make it available to the people of India at reasonable rates.

Neha Smriti, India

Land Tenure

*We rented the land for a bit of fun
To escape from the Rat Race
we had already run
We felt, at that time, that we needed a rest
And leased the land that seemed the best.*

*We bought lots of cows - for dairy and beef
They trampled the grass and ate every leaf
The landscape turned from
bright green to brown,
But we didn't care
'cause we lived in the town.*

*We kept the farm for a year or two
Then gave it back and went on through
We might go out and rent more today
And treat it exactly the very same way.*

Andrew Hobbs, Australia

> ❓ "I can't understand why adults are so stupid to think that technology can solve every single problem. "
>
> *Mauricio Flores Castro, Mexico*

Poisoned *soils*

All our food – except sea life – relies on the soil in one way or another. So for everyone's sake the problem of poisoned and degraded soils must be dealt with as soon as possible.

Tom the Survivor

Once upon a time there was a cattle boy called Tom. The grazing was very poor in that area with dry shrubs and bushes. One summer, Tom and his friends set out to look for water and pasture for the cattle. They walked for six kilometres without finding any. Overgrazing had long since destroyed the grass and strong winds had blown away the fertile topsoil. Tom mused about the past. He wished he had been a chief during those days, able to make sure that the land was properly looked after and that trees were planted. Turning, he saw two cows stumble and fall down dead. The boys cried to their gods for an answer but all in vain. Finally they turned back home through the scorching sunshine to deliver the sad news. Soon, famine broke in the area and many people died. Tom realised he would have to leave his home and go far away to find pasture for his cattle if he was to survive the famine. So he turned sadly and left. *Mutyaba Andrew Kahua, Uganda*

POPs

POPs stands for Persistent Organic Pollutants – that is, poisonous substances that persist – or hang about – in the environment. They come mostly from fertilisers, pesticides and industrial waste. Problems arise because they are taken in by plants and animals which we, or other animals, eat.

Problem down under

In Australia, approximately 30% of our fertile land has been lost in 20 years. This disaster has been caused by two main factors. First, Australian soils cannot tolerate intensive modern farming methods. The soils become dustlike and are often blown away. The second main factor is salinity (saltiness) of the soil. As land is cleared, there are no trees to keep the ever-rising water table at bay. When the water table rises, it carries with it the salt that occurs naturally in the soil. When the water reaches the surface, it evaporates, leaving a salty residue. This makes the land rock hard and useless. Thankfully, the Australian government is backing many landcare projects and farmers have been using satellite technology in order to plan their land reclamation programmes better. They are planting trees, draining the rising water table, building fences to keep animals enclosed and protecting existing patches of bush.

Andrew Hobbs, Australia

Steven Appollo Kalule, Uganda

ℹ Forests - *lungs of the world*

Forests, like oceans, recycle carbon dioxide into oxygen, and provide habitats for most of the world's biodiversity. They are also a vital source of building materials and firewood. But almost all of them are under threat.

Natural Forests

The world has lost 80% of the original forests that covered the earth. The remaining old-growth forests are found mostly in the Amazon rainforest, Central Africa, Southeast Asia, Canada and the Russian Federation. But they are threatened with logging, mining and development.

Deforestation

We are losing forest at a rate of 375 km² a day – an area the size of Greece each year. Causes include urban development, clearance for agriculture, fuel wood collection, timber exploitation, fires and submersion of forests in lakes created by hydro-electric dams. Deforestation contributes to desertification, global warming, poverty and loss of beauty. More than half the Central American rainforest has gone. The Amazon will not last to the end of the 21st century if the current rate of cutting it down continues.

Map: dark green areas show location of the last remaining tropical rainforests

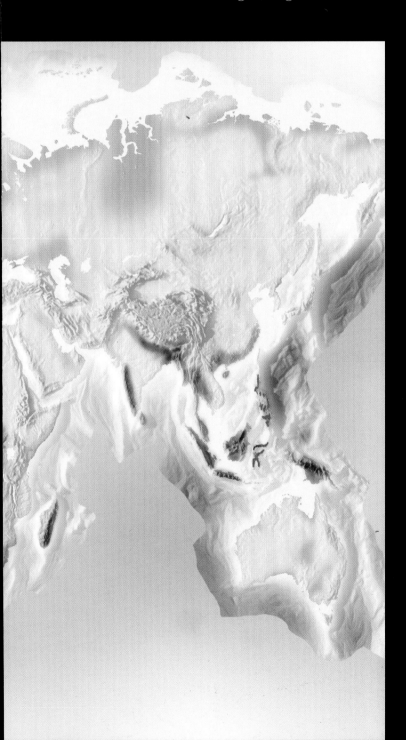

Forest Fires

Fires start from human action or natural causes. In Indonesia and many countries in South America, farmers start most of the forest fires to clear land of trees. Much of the cleared land is used for pasture. The fires in Indonesia in 1997 were featured in the news, but there were bigger fires in Brazil (1997) and Mongolia (1996). Forest fires add carbon dioxide (CO_2) to the atmosphere. In this way, the fires contribute to global warming and the smoke makes whole populations sick.

Sick Forests

Many forests are sick! Air pollution is a main cause: smokestack industries cause acid rain, which attacks forests. In parts of Central and Eastern Europe, you see miles and miles of dead and dying trees. In Africa, drought, civil war, bush fires and inappropriate agricultural practices are degrading forests.

 Rain *forests*

Tropical rainforests hold the greatest diversity of life on the planet. For example, there are five times as many tree species on Madagascar than in the whole of North America. Rainforests are nature's most precious gift.

Losing rainForest

In 1999, the United Nations announced that about 13.7 million hectares of the world's rainforest are cleared or burned each year – about one football pitch every second! Logging of trees for timber, clearing of land for meat production, and mining are ways companies strip the land of trees. Poor people are forced on to forest land because rich companies have squandered the good agricultural land. In Lacandona rainforest in Chiapas, Mexico, one hectare of the forest will have about 30 different species of trees, 50 of orchids, 40 birds, 20 mammals, 300 butterflies and more than 5,000 insects. Now, more than 50% of the rainforest has been destroyed by population growth, industrial development, agriculture, farms and extraction of petroleum. We must preserve the rest.

Ricardo Quintana Vellejo, Mexico and Peris Siamanta Memus, Kenya

" In a tropical country like Indonesia, it is very easy to find wood for paper. We have many trees for that. But imagine the land if it were not replanted. It would look like an old, bald man. *Astri Rahayu, Indonesia* "

Photograph: Tom Jolly, Peru

Silence

lives in the rainforests of the Amazon
Where every drop of cool rain falls
As a thread of gossamer curtain
Parting to reveal a mime:
Spiders spinning life tales
Between giant trees;
Big brown ants readying a rich feast for their queen
Silence walks through this ageing carpet
Of muddy earth and leaves
Through a dark, endless cavern of
Translucent green
Covering each breath with a heavy blanket
of quiet. Even the Earth does not speak
As it claims an old tree
crashing
soundlessly.

Jeneen Garcia, Alexander Bain School, Mexico

Iwokrama Project

The Iwokrama Institute in Guyana is training people locally and internationally to utilise forests without destroying them. In 1989, the government gave 360,000 hectares of its forest to create the Rainforest Research Institute. Since 1996, it has found 12 new species of reptiles and amphibians. Iwokrama has become a natural preserve offering refuge to other animals who need to escape from human activity.

Trevor Benn, Guyana

Temperate *forests*

For millions of years, temperate forests have provided food and shelter for people. Now, we are tearing them down like hooligans, just for money. They are disappearing even faster than the rainforests!

Forests in Russia

Russia has always been called a country of forests. You can find the description in many books, but you should see it. It is beautiful in all seasons. In winter it is like a white fairy tale. Everything is covered with snow. All the trees are white and only fir trees and pine trees are green. In summer the forest is a bright canvas of colours and a beautiful symphony of birds singing. I know that people need things made out of wood but how can we live without this beauty?

Taraskina Anya, Russia

Prayer of the Tree

*On cold nights I am
the heat of your hearth,
I screen you from the sun
with friendly shade
I give people fruits and flowers
As you thirst, my fruits refresh you
I am the beam that holds your house,
The board of your table,
the bed you lie on
The timber that builds your boat
and from which you get furniture.
I am the hands of your hoe,
And the door of your homestead.
The wood of your cradle and the shell
of your coffin.*

Samuel Alodina, Ghana

> " We, the children of today, must demand that laws are passed to control the rate at which forests are cut to ensure that some forest remains for the future. "
>
> *Richard Buobo Mesco, Uganda*

CHiPKO MoVeMeNT

Chipko means "to hug" in an Indian language. In 1730, a Jodhpur Maharaja ordered woodcutters to fetch wood from the Bishnoi region. Bishnois abhor killing – even of trees. Women and the elderly protected the trees by hugging them. 363 Bishnois were killed by the king's loggers before they gave up. Almost 250 years later, the saga was repeated when villagers from Gopeshwar, Uttar Pradesh confronted loggers from a sports goods factory in March 1973, who planned to consume the lovely lush forests on which their lives depended. The villagers rushed to the forests shouting "Chipko! Chipko!" and hugged the trees, daring the loggers to let their axes fall on their backs. These loggers were terrified by them and fled! Thus began one of the world's most famous non-violent conservation movements, the Chipko movement.

B.I.Blah, Shillong, India

IriSH ForeStry

As the last ice age receded, plants began to grow and animals arrived in Ireland. People arrived about 7,000 years ago to find a country covered in woodlands of ash and elm with alder and willow in wet places, oak and holly on acid soil, pine and birch on the mountains.

Slowly forests were cleared for farms, houses, ships and for fuel. By 1920, only 0.5% of the country had forest left. Alarmed, the Irish government started to plant trees. Our planted woodlands contain spruce, larch, fir and pine. There is now over 7% of the country covered with forest. Forestry is very important for our economy and provides much employment.

Togher National School, West Cork, Ireland

Picture: Florencia Ferreyra, Argentina

 Biodiversity

Biodiversity means the rich variety of life forms in nature. GEO warns us that many of the world's different plants and animals are under severe threat of extinction. Many species are lost already.

Loss of Habitat

An ecosystem is a place where nature creates a unique mix of air, water, soil and a variety of living organisms to interact and support each other. Destroy these ecosystems and we are destroying ourselves. Deforestation, overfishing, over-hunting, forest fires, pollution and modern agricultural practices all contribute to the loss of habitat. Cutting roads and railways through habitats blocks natural migration and feeding routes.

Genetic Manipulation

Living organisms are made up of cells. Scientists have found a way to copy, or clone, the information, or genes found in cells to make new plants and animals. But no one knows if it is totally safe to take genes from one species and add them another. Well-known examples of genetic manipulation include Dolly the sheep – the first cloned mammal, and adding the genes of a toad or a spider to vegetables.

WHO KNOWS?

Scientists have recorded 1.75 million species on our planet and estimate another 5 to 100 million unrecorded species! The educated guess stands at 12.5 million.

Exotic Species

Exotic species are animal and plant species that find themselves outside their native habitat. These species cause changes to the ecosystem and sometimes destroy other species native to that ecosystem. For example, zebra mussels came from Europe to the Great Lakes of North America in the ballast of ships. They spread like a plague in the waterways of the continent, attaching themselves to existing mussels and killing them. Breeding quickly, they clog up hydro-electric generators, encrust the hulls of boats and erode pipes in water treatment plants.

EXTINCTIONS

A species is said to be extinct when it has not been seen for over 50 years. Dinosaurs became extinct 65 million years ago but, in the last 50 years, more animals and plants have become extinct, because of hunting and loss of habitat. Globally, many hundreds of species will face extinction in a very few years without intensive conservation, education and environmental management and policy-making.

Foundation for Global Peace and the Environment

On the *way out*

Tigers are just one of the beautiful species of animals that face extinction in the wild if we cannot step up our efforts to conserve their habitat, and protect them from poachers.

Airmail

From: *African Chimpanzee, Endangered Species of the Forest, Africa*

To: *American Chimpanzee, Endangered Species of the Zoo, USA*

Dear Brother Chump,
How are you? How is the American Zoo? I heard rumours from human tourists who say you are covering your beautiful hair with circus clothes! Why? I was so disappointed. In Africa, humans are killing us. We think we are in grave danger. Our homes are destroyed and we have nowhere to go. It looks like you have a small home in the zoo, but we love living in the wild – we want to remain in our forest. Wish you were here. Your brother, Chimp.

Zelalem Getaneh, Ethiopia

DODOS

The dodo was a large bird found on Mauritius, an island in the Indian Ocean. It was like a big turkey with a large beak. Since it had no natural enemies, it had lost the ability to fly. Having no experience of predators, the dodo was easy for the newly arrived European settlers to catch and kill. The rats and pigs they brought with them also killed thousands. By 1680, 80 years after the arrival of Europeans, the last dodo was dead.

> We must take action against those who get satisfaction in driving species to extinction.
>
> *Tuomas Korteinen, Finland*

Gene Piracy

Sri Lanka's biodiversity has been pirated by countries such as Japan and the USA. These countries plunder indigenous plants from the heart of the Sinharaja jungle and ship them out of the country. They then patent the plants which provide herbal remedies for illness and disease, sometimes selling them back to Sri Lankans at a profit for themselves! So Sri Lanka loses out financially and indigenous people who had the knowledge risk losing rare resources. At the Earth Summit in Rio in 1992, many countries signed the Convention on Biological Diversity to outlaw this practice. The USA did not sign the convention.

R.E.P., Sri Lanka
Picture by Ali Abbas Panju, Kenya

Many animals are in danger because people kill them for sport or profit. Can you imagine a world without animals? How can we stop it becoming a reality?

Adriana Saenz & Ariana Morales, Mexico

Stealing Fruit?

In January 1999, hundreds of parrots, toucans and macaws ate fruit from farms in Guyana. In response, the farmers, using government money, poisoned the birds. People are angry because they believe that a foreign company had destroyed the birds' habitat, which had forced the birds to invade the fruit farms.

Trevor Benn, Guyana

Alien *invasion!*

When a new species is introduced to an ecosystem, it is called an exotic or alien species. If the introduced species survives, the results can be disastrous. Without any natural predators, it reproduces unchecked.

A Sugary Story

In Queensland, Australia, sugar cane is one of the main exports. But in 1935, sugar cane was threatened by beetles. Farmers were very concerned. None of the insecticides they tried worked. Finally, the farmers discovered what they believed was the perfect solution – the giant marine toad of Central and South America. This toad *loved* to eat the sugar cane-eating beetle! The toads did such a good job in Australia, they wiped out all the sugar-cane beetles. The toads were still hungry, so they began to eat native insects, fish, amphibians, ground-nesting birds and small mammals. The toad, renamed the cane toad, has no natural enemies and is poisonous. They are reproducing very fast and it is only a matter of time before they spread all over the north of Australia.

Andrew Hobbs, Australia

Take us to your leader!

In Lake Victoria in Africa, 60% of the native fish species have become extinct due to the introduction of the Nile perch. The perch eats smaller fish and upsets the fragile ecosystem.

Mutyaba Andrew Kagwa, Uganda

> " Humans, once considered to be the only creatures wise enough to alter the environment for our convenience, have turned out to be the only ones insane enough to demolish it. "
>
> *Robert Oburta Wanndera, Uganda*

Stop that plant!

The water hyacinth was first spotted floating on a lake in Uganda in 1987. People say this pretty plant came from South America. In ten short years, it has spread like a horror story throughout the lakes and rivers of eastern and southern Africa.

It affects the fishing industry by suffocating fish breeding sites. It chokes the water transport system. As it rots, it affects drinking water and smells disgusting. It provides a breeding site for mosquitoes that carry malaria, snails that bring bilharzia and snakes that bite.

The weed also creeps into hydro-electric plants, wrapping itself around the turbines like some fairy-tale beanstalk. Pulling the weed out by hand is impossible: you need a crane, and snakes and insects tumble out with it. Horrible!

The best chance of defeating the water hyacinth is perhaps a little beetle that eats the weed. Field trials using the beetle are being done in Uganda right now.

Jean Agnes Lutaya, Uganda

Cecilia Weckström, Finland

ⓘ Urbanisation

Though 60 to 70% of people in developing countries live in rural areas, half the total world population now lives in urban areas, drawing their food and natural resources from the surrounding rural areas.

Growth

In 1970, there were only three cities with more than 10 million people. Now there are 32 and three of these have more than 20 million. Rural people move to cities attracted by the promise of work, higher salaries and a better social life. This growth places ever greater pressure on the environment. For example, in Russia and eastern Europe, tens of thousands of people have migrated to cities since 1989, putting a huge strain on both the natural and the built environment.

Pollution

Most cities suffer from noise and air pollution. Experts say that 20% of Europeans are subject to stress from noise. Air pollution also takes its toll on human health. Millions of dollars are spent on health care due to air pollution and many early deaths result from respiratory diseases such as bronchitis and asthma.

Governments should spend part of the fuel tax on cycle lanes and cheaper means of transport. *UNEP International Children's Conference, Eastbourne, UK, 1995*

UrbaN ISSueS

All cities are divided between rich and poor sectors. Business growth and rising numbers of tourists increase the incomes of the rich but the poor see little of the increased wealth. Vast numbers live in shanty towns in cheap, self-made sheds.

There is insufficient clean water or sanitation, few schools, few amenities of any kind. Health suffers first. It is estimated that 100 million people in cities are homeless in both developed and developing countries. Some of the worst polluting industries are likely to be located in poor or racially distinct neighbourhoods.

Water

Water is the single most valuable resource for cities. Many cities are facing a serious shortage of safe drinking water as a result of leaking pipes and pollution from POPs (see page 39). Most city people in developing countries end up boiling their water, or buying bottles. Where piped fresh water is available, it usually only goes to elite residential areas. The poor still have to buy their water through middle men and end up paying more for it than the rich.

Foundation for Global Peace and the Environment, Japan

⚠ The march *of cities*

Many people want to live in cities – but they should remember as they pass through the city gates that, inside, the reality is often squalor, violent crime, dingy high-rise blocks of flats and open sewers.

World population grows at 215,000 a day. In 1999, we reached six billion people. By 2050, there will be many billions more. We'd need to build a city the size of Lima (Peru) every 20 days to house them. Instead, we will expand and merge existing cities, creating mega-cities. Mexico City has grown from 12 to 18 million in 30 years. Jakarta grew 8 million in just 15 years. China's urban population grew from 192 million to 375 million in 16 years. Cities seem destined to just go on growing and growing!

Benedetta Rossi, Italy

The City

The city is a place full of poetry
Filled with eyes and ears
The eyes are each one of
The tiny lights in this city.
Ears are all the walls that keep all secrets
Not to let them out, but
Save them and add beauty
To the walls, full of culture,
Full of stories on the life of those
Who live inside them.
The city also has angels hidden
We can see them
Their mission is to give
Spirit and soul
To the buildings which are old.

City is a word that has a meaning
In each letter.
C is for Culture
I is for Imagination
T is for Talking and
Y is for You
Because You make the city
Shine and be alive.

Cecilia Farfan, Mexico
Picture: Meana Paula, Argentina

Cities - *garbage factories*

Very few cities in developing countries have proper facilities for disposing of solid and human waste. Because cities generate so much of both, this is a huge problem to people's health and the pleasure of living in a city.

Rubbish Matters

We paid a visit to the municipal dump of the city of Guaiba, in Brazil, and saw the people who make a living from sorting the waste. It might seem impossible that people can survive on waste. But of the 40,000 kg of waste thrown away each day in Guaiba alone, 70% could be recycled. Twenty per cent could be used as compost. So, if it was properly sorted, only 10% of the waste would end up in the dustbin.

We are making a campaign, called "Clean City". In this way we will improve the life quality for all in Guaiba and contribute to preventing the pollution of soil and underground water. Rubbish concerns us all!

Niños Periodistas, F. Canez & C. Rodriguez, Guaiba, Brazil

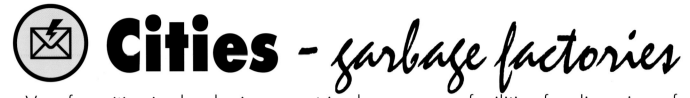

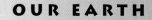

> " 600,000 tons of waste is thrown out in Mexico City every month – enough to fill the vast Aztec football stadium FOUR TIMES! "
>
> *Alexander Bain School, Mexico*

Eco-Task Force, Patna, India

Garbage Mania

In most towns in Zambia, to wake up in the morning, open your window and take a long sniff of that supposedly lovely morning air is a dangerous thing to do – unless you have a gas mask or a blindfold – because both the smell and sight are not pleasant.

We are talking about garbage! It is every-where (except for the richest areas). It is in the homes, streets, schools, parks and work places. You find children playing over it, looking for things to use as toys; you find animals scavenging in it, and hungry people looking in it for a bite to eat. The garbage is never collected properly. It sits and rots and steams and people have to pass through it.

Time and again we complain to our government but they say they have no money and no machinery. In the rainy season, disease spreads fast from the garbage heaps – cholera, dysentery. It is so unhealthy, even migratory birds have stopped visiting us. Something has to be done: there should be laws against throwing unsorted rubbish into the streets; more garbage bins should be provided; low rent districts should have proper garbage collection; recycling plants should be built and the people should be educated about the dangers of garbage. Zambia is a very lovely place but, unless we take action, it will soon be just one big heap of garbage!

Regina Mwansa, Zambia

Polar *regions*

The Arctic and Antartica are called 'Polar Regions'. Both have profound effects on the Earth's climate and ocean systems. Antarctica, a huge land mass as large as the US and Mexico together, is the world's last wilderness.

> " I disagree with any development in Antarctica. Why destroy the only peaceful region of the world? "
>
> *Dominique Mansilla Hermann, Argentina*

THE INUIT

> " We, the Inuit people of the Arctic, are a marine and land-based people. We still rely upon many animal species to support our age-old hunting, fishing, trapping and gathering economy. But many Inuit now use computers and invest in stocks and bonds over the internet. We welcome sustainable development of the Arctic's resources. But we maintain our reverence for Nature and a commitment to treat it with respect. "
>
> *Aqqaluk Lynge of Greenland. President, Inuit Circumpolar Conference, 1997*

Our Polluted Pole

Pollutants are transported to the Arctic by water and air, mainly from Europe, Russia and North America. They are eaten by birds, fish and seals, which in turn are eaten by indigenous people.   *Samuli, Finland*

ℹ️ Polar Facts

- The Southern Ocean is rich in krill and plankton, which form the main source of food for many fish species and whales.
- The Antarctic ozone hole is expected to return annually for many decades.
- Global warming: if the entire Antarctic ice sheet were to melt, it would produce a sea level rise of roughly 60 metres!
- Arctic and Antarctic marine life is threatened by overfishing and hunting.
- Deforestation in the Arctic has affected biodiversity and local climate.
- Norway and Japan are exerting pressure to allow the hunting of whales again. Of a population of 250,000 blue whales in 1900, only 500 remain. In 1994, a sanctuary was created to protect them.

A Wildlife Disaster

When the *Exxon Valdez* crashed in Alaska in 1992, it was a terrible environmental disaster. It disrupted our salmon runs and killed much of our marine life. Many Alaskans helped clean up the oil spill. My father built sea otter clinics as a precaution for future spills and disasters.   *Renée Royal, Alaska, USA*

Now you know the state of our Earth, GEO-2000 reports on all the things that can be done to secure Our Future! It tells what governments are doing at international, national and local levels, what scientists and businesses are doing and then, most important, what WE, the general public, can do - and are doing - to save it!

Our Future

Pull *the strings!*

Pity the poor governments: trying to balance conflicting interests of farmers, trades unions and others on whom they depend for votes. They forget about the poor old planet which can't vote for senior stewards of its environment!

MEAS & CONVENTIONS

MEA stands for Multilateral Environmental Agreement which is when many governments sign an agreement. A convention is when the agreement becomes a Law and thus binding (meaning everyone must obey it!)

MONTREAL PROTOCOL

The Montreal Protocol is an MEA agreed by governments in 1987 to halve Chlorofluorocarbon (CFC) emissions by 1998 and phase them out completely by 2006. A variety of taxes, rules and education programmes were used to implement it. It recognised that rich nations cause more problems and must take a lead. Substitutes for CFCs were researched and a fund was set up to help developing countries change to substitutes. The result is an MEA that serves each nation's interest at a price each can afford. The Montreal Protocol is seen as a successful model for global environmental governance.

SUStaiNaBLe DeveLopMeNt

Meeting the needs of today's generation without compromising the ability of future generations to meet their needs.

Our Common Future, Brundtland Report

Viola Caretti, Italy

"" Whenever you find yourself on the side of the majority, it is time to pause and reflect. ""

Mark Twain

AgeNda 21

A major outcome of the 1992 Earth Summit in Rio de Janeiro, Brazil was a detailed agenda for the 21st Century known as Agenda 21. Governments signed it but it was a 'voluntary agreement' - which means there was no obligation for them to act upon all it contained. Its 40 chapter programme of action covers many aspects of environmental conservation and sustainable development from health to freshwater, oceans, poverty and waste disposal. It has become the guiding document for government management of the environment in most regions of the world: ministers meet every year at the UN Commission for Sustainable Development to check progress on its implementation.

But Agenda 21 isn't complete. Young people identified many gaps, including: war, birth control, human rights, control of multinational corporations, refugees, nuclear disarmament, consumption control, media and renewable energy sources.

 ...and action!

Governments need to put their hearts into controlling environmental degradation and encouraging sustainable lifestyles. Many of them are already doing a lot, but they could all do more. Leaders need to be visionary!

Set up government institutions: A ministry of environment directly responsible for the environment helps to keep environmental issues at the centre of all government planning. Most nations now have them.

Make laws: The obvious way to protect the environment is to make laws against destroying or damaging it. Those who break the laws should be punished with fines or imprisonment.

Implement and enforce laws: If you have laws, you have to enforce them with police and law courts.

Public participation: Local people are more likely to have an understanding of their environmental problems and solutions than distant institutions. So involving the public in decision-making and allowing them access to information will generally result in quicker and more appropriate responses to issues.

Regional cooperation: Regional groups can often work more quickly and effectively to deal with regional problems.

Intelligent prices: It would make sense to tax things that pollute the environment and give financial assistance, called subsidies, to things that do not. But many governments do the reverse by subsidising things that pollute!

Promote new technology: Governments can do more to make industry pay for pollution it creates and encourage new non-polluting technologies.

Deal with social issues: Poverty, population growth and social behaviour get to the root causes of environmental degradation. Investing in solutions to social issues helps the environment.

Here are some ideas GEO-2000 suggests our leaders should focus on:

Combine land and water management. One department integrating land and water management together with social and economic issues would ensure more balanced decision-making.

Change to cleaner technology that does not pollute air or water. Technology exists to reduce pollution – let's use it!

Decrease energy use through energy and carbon taxes. Make those who use more, pay more. Switch to pollution-free technology.

More action to protect forests through research, education, sustainable forest management, more protected areas with benefits going to the local community and eco-tourism.

Play fair. Public money is often provided as an incentive to individuals and companies to produce goods and services. This money is called a subsidy. The goal of governments should be to stop the subsidies which have a negative effect on the environment and which encourage individuals and companies to be wasteful.

Manage water resources for agriculture. Improve awareness and provide loans and incentives to help farmers repair leaks and switch to more efficient irrigation systems.

Idir Kerkouche, Algeria

⚠ **If we** *ruled the world...*

Statements from UNEP and other youth conferences show that young people everywhere want more environmental education, more involvement in decision-making and for us to *think* globally and *act* locally.

GreeN FiRe!

Hi there! 30 enthusiastic young people from all over the world launched the UNEP Youth Advisory Council on February 1 1999 in Nairobi, Kenya at the 'Green Fire' event. Our goal is to exchange ideas and lobby for international agreements. We have UNEP's authority to speak at environmental meetings. Twelve advisors, two from each region, were elected to represent the Council. UNEP has asked us to create a Youth Strategy for Sustainable Consumption – find ways to persuade young people to cut down on their consumption and favour sustainably produced products. If you have any ideas on this, or any other environmental concern, the YAC wants to hear from you. Let's work together to build a healthy future!   *Celine Schwob, France, on behalf of the Youth Advisory Council, contact: theodore.oben@unep.org*

Martina Rizza, Italy

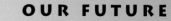

Education

Environmental education should be compulsory and should include:

- a requirement for all graduating students to demonstrate understanding of sustainable development
- action projects in primary schools
- getting students involved in local environmental decision-making
- optional exam courses
- students teaching about environment in partnership with teachers.

Youth Councils

Each country should have a Youth Environment Security Council to look at environmental issues and suggest what action the government should take. The council would also develop projects for young people to carry out, with government support. Representatives of the national councils could meet to exchange ideas and lobby for international agreements to protect the environment for their, and future, generations.

The Editors of Pachamama

Commitments

[From the statement of the UNEP Global Youth Forum, Washington DC 1994]

As young, caring citizens of this planet, we commit ourselves to restoring and preserving our world, and to rebuilding our dreams of tomorrow – pure waters, vast wildlands, clean air and cities free from poverty. We embrace these ten commitments:

1. **Natural resource utilisation:** We must display wisdom and creativity in preserving resources for future generations.
2. **Biodiversity:** We will protect the web of life – its diversity and habitats – and support the preservation of all life on Earth.
3. **Atmosphere:** We will protect it. It is the skin of our planet!
4. **Water:** Water is the nurturer of all terrestrial and aquatic life. We will clean it, protect it and ensure free and fair access for all.
5. **Energy:** We will end wastage of it, conserve it better and seek alternative sources of energy.
6. **Waste:** Waste is a poison in the heart of the global ecosystem. We will reduce, re-use and recycle our waste.
7. **Sustainable living:** We will live in harmony with our ecosystems.
8. **Cooperation and education:** We will build a global community based on fair trade and free transfer of technology.
9. **Human rights:** We will not be intimidated by our apparent lack of power. Together we will act for change. It is our human right.
10. **ACTION!** Above all, we commit ourselves to action. For the fate of the Earth lies not in government hands but in ours.

ℹ️ Emerging *issues*

In the 20th century, human beings learned how to destroy the Earth in two ways: 1) quickly, through a nuclear war; 2) slowly, through environmental destruction. Never was the study of the 'future' more important!

> ❝ Governments need to open their eyes to the needs of the planet and take drastic action for change. At present, they are blinded by power struggles and distorted priorities and they are hurting the Earth and themselves. ❞
>
> *Amy Saunders, Scotland*

Looking ahead

What is an emerging issue? Simple! An issue that is emerging! Something that is not yet an issue that everyone is concerned about but which is shortly going to be an immense headache to us all. After getting this far in this book, you will have a fairly good idea about what these are – but it is useful to focus your mind on what scientists and others feel are the most important emerging issues. We have also made a survey of those that young people and various famous people feel are important.

AND THAT PLANET OF POLLUTION WAS CALLED EARTH

Juan Manuel Torreblanca, Mexico

GEO-2000 defines three kinds of emerging issues:

1. Surprises

Something that was not expected by anyone. The past is littered with things that have taken people off-guard when they were least expecting them! For example, no one expected the effects of acid rain on the environment at the start of the Industrial Revolution.

2. Neglected issues

Problems may be well known but ignored for political, economic or social reasons. For example, experts warned that draining water from the rivers flowing into the Aral Sea to irrigate cotton crops would cause the sea to dry up but this was ignored because others wanted to make money.

3. Existing problems

These are things we already know about but which are not yet bad enough to cause serious concern. For example, chemicals sealed in containers and dumped in the sea may be fine for a while – until they begin to leak!

ⓘ What *scientists say*

Where the environment is concerned, the entire GEO project is about trying to understand the future consequences of our actions today. Let's start where governments start – with the scientists. After all, they are the experts!

OceaN FLip-FLop

You thought global warming would just warm up the planet, right? Wrong! If the Arctic ice caps melt, it could very well produce another ice age in northwest Europe. This would happen because cold water flowing south from the Arctic would slow, and possibly halt, the warm Gulf Stream current which now allows people in Scotland to grow palm trees along the coast. If that current is cut off and only cold water reaches Britain's coasts, land temperatures would plummet, there could be permafrost in Europe, and the River Rhine would freeze over. Crop yields would suffer; the transport network could close down for several months a year, and life in northern Europe as we know it could all but disappear.

> " When poverty over-rides everything else, people forget about the environment. "
>
> *Ayub Osman, Kenya*

HELP!

In preparing GEO-2000, more than 200 environmental experts from 50 countries were asked to identify environmental issues that they expect to be on the national and inter-national agendas of governments in the early decades of the 21st century. These are some of the issues with the percent-age of scientists that mentioned them:

Climate change	51%
Freshwater scarcity	29%
Deforestation/ desertification	28%
Freshwater pollution	28%
Poor governance	27%
Loss of biodiversity	23%
Population growth and movements	22%
Changing social values	21%
Contamination from waste disposal	20%
Air pollution	20%
Soil deterioration	18%
Chemical pollution	16%
Urbanisation	16%
Ozone depletion	15%
Energy consumption	15%
Emerging diseases	14%
Natural resource depletion	11%
Food insecurity	11%
Industrial emissions	10%
Natural disasters	7%
War & conflict	7%
Invasive species	6%
Genetically modified organisms	6%
Ocean flip-flop	5%

War!

Nobel laureate, Joshua Lederberg, believes the third world war has already begun – between humans and microbes! Epidemics now spread fast around the world, with one million people a day crossing borders. GEO calls this a 'low probability / high consequence' emerging issue. In other words, when new epidemics break out, like AIDS, the consequences are devastating. Like war itself, prevention is always the best course.

Hassan al Saleh, Oman

What *others think*

We asked our youth contributors to list their top 10 positive emerging trends and top 10 negative ones. We also asked some experts their opinion. Here are the results. What would you add?

Top 10 positive emerging trends

Increased recycling

More reforestation

Greater animal protection

More use of solar energy

Water conservation

Higher environmental awareness

More measures against pollution

More power to NGOs

More natural food products

More protection of rainforests

Top 10 negative emerging trends

Increased pollution

More deforestation

Intensified hunting of animals

More air pollution

Widening ozone hole

Worse water pollution

Water scarcity

More toxic waste

Over-population

Increased amounts of rubbish

WHat do you tHiNK?

"We have to make a decision about the use of nuclear power. Can we run the risk of more accidents, like Chernobyl, devastating the environment." Would you like to see a world without nuclear weapons and nuclear power plants at the end of your life?

Julia Ivanchenka, Ukraine

...aNd about tHiS?

"Dumping rubbish anywhere, anyhow, has become a habit in African cities today." We are running out of places to dump our garbage. How can we force our generation to re-use, recycle and repair their possessions to achieve the most important goal which is to *reduce* the amount of garbage they generate?

Jennifer Chanda, Zambia

" Inside every big issue lurk hundreds of little issues that may, in the end, emerge and do more damage to the environment than the big one. In climate change, it is small issues like El Niño that do the damage. Marie Curie thought she had made a great discovery with radium but she could not foresee that radiation sickness would kill her. No one knows what will emerge. **"**

Jukka Uosukainen,
Deputy Director, International Affairs,
Ministry of the Environment, Finland

" The most critical issue we shall be dealing with in the next century is precisely the same one that we failed to deal with in this one: human greed. As long as we sanctify greed as a noble human motive, we cannot overcome hunger, poverty and oppression or redress the consequences of our own remorseless drive to exploit for our own good the environment and life-style of other people's cultures. **"**

John le Carré, Author, England, UK

Sidiono Ra, Indonesia

" More and more ordinary people are talking of peace. As an ageing optimist I believe that the day of the peace child may be dawning – peace with the Earth and amongst all people who want to share, not destroy, its bounty. The green renaissance is here. "

David Bellamy, Naturalist, England, UK

" I have never in my whole life been a pessimist. I would never have given a billion dollars to the UN if I didn't think we were capable of doing something about these problems. But we have to act now. If we wait another 10 to 15 years, it will be too late. Population growth, climate change, mass extinction – are like snow-balls rolling down a steep slope. Our challenge is to stop them before they become avalanches. "

Ted Turner, philanthropist & founder of Cable News Network, USA

" The tension between high and rising consumption and decreasing resources is likely to become the key environmental problem in the next century. The pressure of poor people on resources is often highlighted but the rich consume more: their food, houses, clothes, cars, lifestyles are all resource intensive. We will need fairer access to resources and that will mean placing curbs on how much the rich consume. "

Sir Shridath Ramphal, former Secretary-General of the Commonwealth, Guyana

" Mindless growth should be considered guilty until proven innocent. Do we need it? Can we afford it? "

David Brower, Earth Island Institute, USA

" My concerns are chiefly -
 • The impact of micro-pollutants on human
   health in ways that we cannot possibly
   predict.
 • Genetic engineering, both for agricultural
   and environmental reasons. We are likely
   to be swamped by the genetics revolution.
   We totally lack the moral and ethical
   values and institutions to judge the
   benefits of all the new products and
   technologies.
 • Bio-terrorism: unscrupulous terrorist
   organisations may get more sophisticated
   in their use of biological weapons.
 • Ever larger numbers of young people in
   both developed and developing worlds
   will end up with no gainful purpose in life
   or means of earning a livelihood.

Jonathon Porritt, Programme Director,
Forum for the Future, England, UK "

" Deterioration of the environment
   and global resources in combination
with growing disparities between the
rich and poor are going to force us to
change our way of life. We may be able to
party on for another half century or so, but
I'm afraid that our societies will then be
thrown into disrepair. Our situation right
now is rather like that of a man who jumps
off the Empire State Building and, as he
passes the 9th floor window, smiles and
waves, saying, 'So far so good!' Very soon,
we are going to hit the limits of the
Earth's carrying capacity, and when that
issue emerges, it will hurt us all.

Herman Verheij, Policy Advisor, Ministry of
Environment, the Netherlands

Ahmed Egan, Maldives

The Future

What does the future hold for us?
Smog filled skies and poison cars
And broken land with useless dust
And Nature's beauty behind bars.

Can I ever show my children
(If they ever come my way)
The beauty of a sunset
At the ending of the day?

Can I walk into a forest
And surround myself with trees
Yet know that it will remain
For me to visit as I please?

Can I sit upon the seashore
And breathe in salty air,
Or will it be so dirty
That it is unsafe to be there?

I know that I can today
Do all the things I've said
But when today is yesterday
Will all these things be dead?

This problem is enormous
As we gradually take heed,
So we must fix it quickly,
Using words and thoughts and deeds.

Write a letter, start a group
Or do something that seems small
For whatever is done to aid the Earth
Is fantastic for us all.

If we save what's there before us
So it'll be there when we go,
Then we'll leave a gift more precious
Than our kids will ever know.

Andrew Hobbs, Australia

What

we can do

⚠ **What** *you can do!*

Children are often the driving force behind eco-friendly living. Trouble is, as teenagers, they are the targets of massive advertising campaigns that urge them to consume voraciously and drop their eco-friendly ideals.

COMMiTMeNtS...

Things you can do to protect the environment every day, wherever you are!

- Don't leave your rubbish lying around.
- Support conservation campaigns eg: Adbusters, No shopping days, Trash free lunches, Greenpeace...
- Get your family and school thinking about environment issues daily!
- Start a *Pachamama* Club – or horticultural, bird, hiking or nature club.
- Get traffic out of residential areas!
- Do environmental assemblies at your school. Celebrate Earth Day (*22nd April*) and World Environment Day (*5th June*)
- Plant trees – care for and nurture them
- Get your community to encourage recycling of all their waste
- Promote anti-pollution awareness: demand car-free days
- Create a garden! Grow fruits and vegetables. Reward yourself with nature's riches every day!

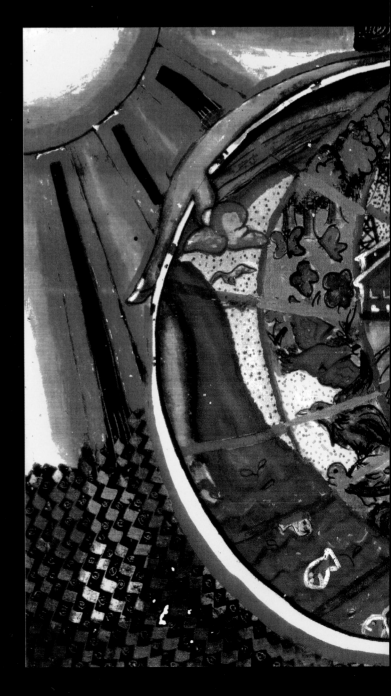

PLant a tree!

Plant a tree for every happy moment.
Recycle paper for every feeling you wrote.
Take care of endangered animals for
everyone you love. **"**

*Monica Edward, Monica Ortega
& Roxana Nevorrez, Mexico*

...on for Global Peace and the Environment, Japan

Peace Child

Peace Child is a youth-led
organisation of some 500 youth
eco-groups in 120 countries. Its goal
is to enable young people to
communicate vital global issues to
each other and to adults. Set up in
1981, it used the platform of a
musical play to allow young people
to communicate powerfully their
fears about the threat of nuclear war.

Environment and sustainability
issues are now the focus. Peace
Child uses the platform of books,
educational materials, newsletters
and conferences to enable young
people around the world to work
together to communicate their
feelings on these issues to adults and
government officials.

They created *Rescue Mission* – a
children's Agenda 21. On its success
and royalties, young people designed
and built a residential Sustainable
Development Training Centre where
young people from all over the world
run the office and manage projects
like this one. Similar centres are now
being set up in Ghana, Guyana and
Senegal. Come and join us!

*For information, contact:
www.oneworld.org/peacechild*

Eco Times

millennium issue December 1999

Paper Tiger!

Kruti Parekh, 13, from India promotes environmental awareness through her magic show which she has performed 1700 times. In it, she eats waste paper and produces an endless sheet of recycled paper from her mouth. She also promotes worms! Yes, worms – the great unsung heroes of the eco-movement. Put them in any bin of compostable rubbish and they will break it down into rich fertiliser in days. Kruti calls it "The 2 in 1 process – waste disposal and fertiliser manufacture all in one!"   *fax: + 91 22 369 8457*

Life's a clean beach!

Grupo Sawite from Lima, Peru find their beaches a haven for dumping garbage and waste. The Grupo volunteers clean the beaches and educate their community about the effects of pollution on marine life and human health. *e-mail: grupo@pucp.edu.pe*

RAP for the planet!

Right Angle Productions (RAP) uses video to enable young people to voice their concerns. RAP workshops teach young people how to use the video camera. RAP uses video to link young people from England with a village in Zimbabwe, through music, workshops and discussions of human rights, environment etc. RAP will soon have a website to allow the world to watch them actively doing things to save the planet. *RAP, Union Street Centre, Union St. OXFORD OX4 1LJ, UK*

South Africa!

The new South Africa cares for its environment and actively involves young people! The Wilger Veld Youth Club has organised community clean-ups in several townships afflicted by poverty and a lack of facilities. In one, Tamboville, a community food garden was started and now they all have fresh produce. Through raising awareness, people now put rubbish in bins and wetland birds are returning.

e-mail: merns-kf@acaleph.vista.ac.za

A breath of air

Students of Apeejay School in India got fed up with the air pollution caused by cars. Air pollution causes chronic lung disease in 12% of Indian children. One morning, a group of high school students stood at a busy intersection in South Delhi and flagged down vehicles to check pollution control certificates. Those who had one got a handwritten thank you note. Those who did not were politely directed to a testing centre or faced a fine the next day.

Solar Visions

Imagine cooking for the rest of your life for free! Never collecting fire wood, never paying a fuel bill. Solar box cookers offer this. A group of Finns from a school in Helsinki have set up a link with schools in Namibia to introduce them to solar cookers. Every year, they take cookers designed by the best Finnish solar engineers to Namibia and show local Namibian young people how to make and use them themselves. *Contact: Monika Sandell, fax: + 358 9 1480 2498*

Yes to eco-action!

A group of students in California felt that, if their teachers would not teach them about environmental issues, they should do it themselves. So they trained themselves and then toured their region doing trainings and seminars on environmental issues. Each summer, they do a Youth Jam where they bring together youth environmental leaders to discuss strategies and make new plans.
e-mail:levanasa@hotmail.com

Paradise in the city

In 1991, an Environmental Youth Alliance developed an organic youth garden in an abandoned lot in Vancouver. Their goal is sustainable food production in a crowded urban environment. Food is grown there to supplement the group's diets. Trees, flowers and herbs are also grown. The garden is used by many people. Passers-by are encouraged to stroll through it and learn from it.

EYA, Box 34097 Vancouver, B.C. V6J 4MI

Kenya's Kicking!

'Think locally' is the rallying call for a group of young Kenyans. Planting trees, collecting garbage, surveying plants and wildlife in the nearby mountains – this group does not believe in waiting for things to happen. 'We plant trees, conserve wildlife and educate people', says Anthony Kaiseiyie, 16. 'The rains last year swept soil to the ocean. Planting trees and cover crops like sweet potatoes cuts down soil loss.'

e-mail:k97sw01@kzoo.edu

Say ....treeeeeeees!

Students from the Eco-Teens group in Indonesia use compost from local rubbish and seeds gathered in local forests to replant deforested areas. Each member of the group takes a seed, plants it in a poly-bag and cares for it like a pet! Once the seed has grown and is ready to move, they plant it out in a community where there are not many trees. Then, they start all over again with a new seed.

e- mail: p_risa@hotmail.com

Plastic Fantastic!

The Khoslo Nature Club from Trashigang organised a plastic collection competition to raise awareness of the fact that 4800 pieces of plastic are thrown away each month by their small community of 800 people. The sacks of plastic were put on display to the public and prizes were awarded to the students. It's great! We don't see nearly as much plastic around now, and nearly everyone goes shopping with a cloth bag.

Trashigang, Bhutan

A class act

In the Sultanate of Oman, the "Green Beans" a local youth environmental group, have been working so hard it's a wonder they have time for their studies! "We raise money by organising sales and after school movie shows", says Hassan Al Saleh, 17. Hassan told us the money is used to buy acres of rain forest and adopt endangered animals. Twice a year, the Green Beans hold a beach clean-up. "We have come a long way in raising awareness in and out of school. If we all work together, we can make this world a better place."

Kids for the reef

Forty scuba divers from all over the Philippines organised a clean-up programme for the reefs in Batangas, south of Manila. "Kids for the Reef" drew young people into the project collecting waste along the shoreline. The programme made young people aware of how fragile Philippine reefs are. Of 500 known coral species, 400 are found in the Philippines. That's 400 good reasons to get involved!
e-mail: byte@planet.net.ph

PlanetXpress

Amy Saunders, 19, from Scotland, UK, is developing a website for young people on global issues. "Planet Xpress is a place to meet people from all over the world, exchange ideas and take positive action," says Amy. "It is run by and for young people. We need more young contributors, web-designers, out-reachers and co-ordinators. Please get in touch!" *website: www.planetxpress.org*

Power rangers

Essau Lower school in the Gambia has a group of 13 to 14-year-old boys who collect used batteries and move them to a safe site. "We realised that batteries were being dumped all over," said one of them. "Young people are not aware of the health dangers they bring. We are extending this new project to many schools and eventually the whole area."

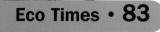

How green are you?!

20 questions - Have you ever...

Answer Score

1. separated the trash into organic / inorganic, paper / plastic etc? ....
2. taken your paper, metals etc. for recycling? ....
3. left lights on after you have left a room in your house? ....
4. organised a youth environmental group in your school area? ....
5. tried to educate people in your neighbourhood about eco-issues? ....
6. allowed your dog to defecate in a public area? ....
7. watched a parent use dangerous chemicals on the soil and not stopped them? ....
8. burned rubbish in your garden on a sunny day? ....
9. got your parent to drive you less than a kilometre to school / to a friend? ....
10. done clean-ups on lakes and rivers in your local area? ....
11. built habitats for wild animals in your garden or local park? ....
12. joined Greenpeace, WWF or another eco-organisation? ....
13. planted trees, flowers or edible landscaping in your community? ....
14. campaigned against cruelty to animals or hunting? ....
15. organised an environmental meeting at your school? ....
16. been on a demonstration about an environmental issue? ....
17. lobbied your local council, written letters etc, on an environmental issue? ....
18. used your bicycle or your legs instead of a car? ....
19. persuaded your parents to improve the insulation in your home? ....
20. got your parents to buy low-energy light bulbs, high-efficiency appliances? ....

TOTAL ....

Answer each of the above questions: a=always; b=very often; c=sometimes; d=not often; e=never. Put your answers in the first column on the right. In the second column write your score for each question as follows:
– for questions 1, 2, 4, 5, 10, 11, 12, 13, 14, 15, 16, 17, 18, 19, 20:
a = 5; b = 4; c = 3; d = 2; e = 0
– for questions 3, 6, 7, 8, 9:
a = 0; b = 2; c = 3; d = 4; e = 5

Ikramah Jafar, Seychelles, Africa

ReSULtS

Total up your score and calculate your green-ness!

80 – 100: you are so *green*, people might think you're coming down with something! But congratulations! You are clearly living very lightly on the planet! Keep up the good work and spread the word.

69 – 79: Not bad! Probably room for improvement in your personal life and there's sure to be more you could do in your community environment.

40 – 59: Many of us editors fell into this category. We are all basically lazy! It's time to get your hands dirty. Turn that TV off, get off that couch, get out and DO SOMETHING!

20 – 39: you are dangerously close to being a problem to your planet and your community. The environment is clearly not a priority for you. So go back, read this book again and THINK about the consequences of going on as you are: dead planet, right!

0 – 19: you are shaping up to be a dangerous planetary vandal! You should read this book once a day and twice on Thursdays and do 3 environmental clean-ups every day before breakfast! Wear green, paint your house – and your face – green. BE GREEN!

Contributors List

With many thanks to the following groups and individuals who made contributions to this book:

Asia & the Pacific

Samtse Junior High School, Trashigang Bhutan
Eco-Task Force, Patna, Bihar, India
Kruti's Eco Foundation, Maharastra, India
SHRUSIT, Tukum Chandrapur, India
Tamil Nadu United Nations Association, Chennai, India
Eco-teen's Club, Sukabumi, Indonesia
ECO-NEPAL, Katmandu, Nepal
Yangrima Environment Group, Kathmandu, Nepal
Urjana Shrestha, Kathmandu, Nepal
Pakistan Environmental Lobbying Society, Lahore, Pakistan
Khwaka's, Peshawar, Pakistan
Peace Child, Las Piñas City, Philippines
Jose Enrique I. Luciano, Philippines
Ermiza Tegal, Mankola, Sri Lanka
R.E.P., Mankola, Sri Lanka
Andrew Hobbs, Australia
Ling So Low, Malaysia

Africa

M.S. Planète Terre, Ouidah, Benin
Ndjama Benjamin, Shell Cameroon Dla, Cameroon
Environmental Management Forum, Yaounde, Cameroon
Rescue Mission, Douala, Cameroon
SOS High School, Awassa, Ethiopia
Rescue Mission, Banjul, Gambia
Bakotek Lower Basic School, Gambia
Accra Academy Rescue Mission, Accra, Ghana
Ashanti Goldfields Company Primary School, Ashanti, Ghana
Deks School Rescue Mission, Tema, Ghana
Bulaago Youth Environmental Project, Ghana
Colibri Wildlife Club, Mahe, Seychelles
The Ebonite Foundation, Nigeria
Bank School, Kampala, Uganda
Desk School Rescue Mission, Ghana
Kinbu Secondary School, Tech Branch of Gunsa, Accra, Ghana
Rescue Mission, Tema, Ghana
African Environmental Education Foundation, Nairobi, Kenya
Ayub Osman, Nairobi, Kenya
Enkii Primary School, Nairobi, Kenya

Projet Intègre de Keita (FAO), Keita, Niger
Daniel Onyi Eboh, Nsukka, Nigeria
Nigeria Society for the Improvement of Rural People, Nsukka, Nigeria
Life – Link / Rescue Mission, Akwa Ibom State, Nigeria
YIELD, Owerri, Nigeria
P.C.I. Azania Secondary School, Dar es Salaam, Tanzania
Joint Energy and Environment Project (JEEP), Kampala, Uganda
The Pogis, Kampala, Uganda
Allan Kiwala, Rescue Mission, Local Council 1 Kasubi 2, Kampala, Uganda
Mutyaba Andrew Kagwa, Nyenga Minor Seminary, Kampala, Uganda
Clac Sylver Nanyumba, UNEP & Rescue Mission, Kampala, Uganda
Wildlife Club, Kampala, Uganda
St. Pontiano Ngondwe's Secondary School, Kampala, Uganda
Bullaago Youth Environment Project, Mbale, Uganda
Kireka Youth Group, Kampala, Uganda
Mutaki Charles, City Secondary School, Kampala, Uganda
Kalule Apollo Steven, City Secondary School, Kampala, Uganda
Mubiru Benjamin, Rescue Mission, Kampala, Uganda
Rescue Mission Makarere University, Uganda
Mwiri Writer's Club, Jinja, Uganda
Rescue Mission Uganda
Met Society, Kampala, Uganda
Jean Agnes Lutaaya, Rescue Mission, Kampala, Uganda
Wild Life Club, Nsambya, Uganda
Wilger Veld & Youth club, Gauteng, South Africa
Independent Earth Conservation Volunteers, Lusaka, Zambia
Mission Terre, Algerie
Ahmed Egan, Maldives
Peace Child, Sierra Leone

Latin America & the Caribbean

Asociación Ecoboy, Lima, Perú
Asociación Pukllasunchis, Cusco, Perú
Escuela N°23 Almafuerte, Lavallol, Buenos Aires, Argentina
Escuela N° 37 "Bernardino Rivadavia" de Esteban
     Echeverría, Buenos Aires, Argentina
Escuela N°66 SES Quincentenario de la Independencia
Lavallol, Buenos Aires, Argentina
Embajada para la Preservación y Conservación de la
     Naturaleza, Jujuy, Argentina
Instituto Grilli, Monte Grande, Buenos Aires, Argentina
Instituto de Enseñanza Secundaria Saúl Taborda,
     Córdoba, Argentina
Misión Rescate Argentina
Misión Rescate Mendoza, Argentina,
Noelia V. Cocco, Luis Guillón, Buenos Aires, Argentina
Taller Chicos Cariló, Buenos Aires, Argentina
Team Work, Buenos Aires, Argentina
Pamela Castro, Moreno, Buenos Aires, Argentina
The Grandson's Mass, Bauxita, Brazil
Ceciell, Guaiba, Brazil
Julio Cesar de Souza Reis, Bauxita, Brazil
Association of Youth, Georgetown, Guyana
St. George's College Environmental Group,
     Kingston, Jamaica
Grupo Scout 55 Coyoacan, Guadalupe, Mexico
Grupo Alexander Bain, Mexico City, Mexico
The American School of Asuncíon, Asuncíon, Paraguay
Grupo Saywite – PUCP, Lima, Peru

North America

E. Mayo, Ontario, Canada
Marie – Clarie Segger, Canada
Quluaq School, Clyde River, Northwest Territories, Canada
Environmental Youth Alliance, Vancouver, Canada
Rescue Mission Group, Spruce Glen School,
     Huntsville, Canada
Daniel P Maynchan, Hertford, USA
Gideon Welles School, Glastonbury, USA
Ke Ala Hoku, Hawaii, USA
Youth for Environmental Sanity, Santa Cruz, California

West Asia

United Nations, Economic and Social Commission
     for Western Asia, Beirut, Lebanon
Kuwait National Commission for Education Science
     & Culture, Safat, Kuwait
The Royal Society for the Conservation of Nature,
     Amman, Jordan
The Sultan's School, Seeb, The Sultanate of Oman

Europe & Central Asia

Leen Labeeuw, Ghent, Belgium
Prva Bosnjacka Bimnazija, Sarajevo, Bosnia Herzegovina
Clean Water, Sofia, Bulgaria
UNESCO Club, Olomouc, Czech Republic
8B – Yläaste, Oulu, Finland
Kari Koistinen, Rovaniemi, Finland
Green Circle / Kimitoöns Gymnasium, Kimito, Finland
Minna Pesonen, Helsinki, Finland
Puolalanmäki School – Agenda 21 group, Turku, Finland
S.M.S. G. Falcone – P. Borsellino School, Milan, Italy
First Children's Embassy in the World, Skopje, Macedonia
ECO US, Krakow, Poland
Trofimova Marina, Saratov, Russia
Physico technical Lyceum W1, Saratov, Russia
UNESCO Club, Piran, Slovenia
Jose Damien Gonzalez, Luzern, Switzerland
Millbrook School, Cornwall, UK
St. Joan of Arc School, Rickmansworth, UK
Waste Not Education, London, UK
Ecologist of Mariinskaya Gymnasium, Odessa, Ukraine
Oaklands Primary School, Aberdare, Wales, UK
Togher National School, Ireland
Amy Saunders, Scotland, UK

With many thanks to the Foundation for Global Peace and the Environment, Tokyo, Japan *(Secretary General: Tomoko Yano)* for the use of several winning paintings from their annual Environmental Art Contest.

Also a great Thank You to all those who through their hard work and contacts helped spread the word about this project all over the world!

ANDES — Major mountain range in South America, which passes through seven countries

ACIDIFICATION — Process by which soil or water becomes acidic

AFFORESTATION — Planting trees and plants

AIDS — Acquired Immune Deficiency Syndrome: often fatal. Infection is spread through sexual intercourse, blood transfusion or sharing of hypodermic needles. There is no known cure

ALIEN — Something which is foreign

AMPHIBIAN — Living both on land and in water

ANTARCTIC — A continent in the south polar region

AQUIFER — Layer of rock or soil under the ground that holds water – like a big underground sponge

ARCTIC — (Of) the north polar regions

ASTHMA — Illness which makes breathing difficult

ATMOSPHERE — Layers of air, composed of gases and particles, surrounding the Earth

BALLAST — Weights placed in the hulls of ships to make them more stable

BILHARZIA — Tropical water-borne parasite (flatworm) that enters the bloodstream causing diarrhoea, vomiting, liver and kidney failure and sometimes death

BILLION — A thousand million

BIRTH CONTROL — Methods of preventing pregnancy

BIODIVERSITY — The variety of plants and animals that exist in nature

BRONCHITIS — A disease which affects lungs and breathing

CADMIUM — A chemical element and a soft, silvery white metal. Causes severe illness and even death if inhaled. Used in plating and in making alloys.

CARBON DIOXIDE — Gas formed by burning of carbon and by breathing

CHERNOBYL — Nuclear Power plant near Kiev, Ukraine, which released large amounts of radiation into the atmosphere due to an explosion and fire in the reactor in 1986

CHOLERA — Infectious, often fatal, disease of the digestive system, acquired by drinking contaminated water

CITES — Convention on International Trade in Endangered Species of flora and fauna

CLONE — A genetically identical copy

COMPLIANCE — To act to ensure that the terms of laws are met

CONSERVATION — Preserving the environment

CONSUMPTION — Purchase and use of goods

CONVENTION — An agreement between states

CROPS — Food plants grown for human use

CROP YIELD — The amount of crops produced in a growing cycle

CRUSTACEANS — Aquatic animals with hard shells like crab, lobster and shrimp

DEFORESTATION — Clearing forests of trees

DEGRADATION — When things are worn away, reduced, damaged

DESERTIFICATION — Where land starts to turn into desert

DEVELOPED COUNTRIES — Rich countries, sometimes referred to as "the north"

DEVELOPING WORLD — Poor countries, sometimes referred to as "the south"

DYSENTERY — Infection of the large intestine

EARTH SUMMIT — A world summit held in Rio de Janeiro in 1992 on environment and development

EL NIÑO — A naturally occurring ocean condition resulting in major changes in weather and biological productivity

EDIBLE LANDSCAPING — Planting trees/shrubs that produce fruits and vegetables which can be eaten by the public

ENVIRONMENT — Everything around us, plants, air, land, life etc.

EPIDEMIC — A disease which attacks many people at about the same time

EUTROPHICATION The addition of nutrients to waters caused by rain water washing off excess fertiliser from agricultural land and human waste from settlements. Water plants flourish on these nutrients and oxygen in the water is depleted

EXOTIC SPECIES Animals or plants introduced to new environments different from where they originated; may be dangerous to native species

EXXON VALDEZ An oil tanker which went aground causing huge environmental destruction in Alaska in 1992

FAMINE Extreme lack of food

FATALITY Death

FERTILITY Capable of producing new life = fertile

FERTILISER Substance which provides plant nutrients when added to soil

FOOD SECURITY Knowing that you have enough food

FURNACITE Processed coal for use in domestic fires

GEO REPORT Global Environment Outlook

GENE Part of a cell that all living things inherit from their parents that determines their characteristics

GENETIC ENGINEERING A scientific technique which alters the genes of an organism. Used in medicine, industry and agriculture

GENETICALLY MODIFIED Something which has been altered through genetic engineering

GENERIC Belonging to a large group rather than a specific individual; describing something in a general, rather than in a specific, way

GREENPEACE An international NGO which campaigns on environmental issues

HABITAT Natural home of plant or animal

HEAVY METALS Metals of high density which are often toxic to human health

HECTARE 100 metres x 100 metres

HERBAL REMEDIES Using herbs and plants to cure illnesses

HYPODERMIC Introducing medical remedies or drugs under the skin

HOOKWORM A small worm that enters the human body through the skin and then lives in the intestines.

IMPLEMENTATION To put something into action

INCA The people who lived in Peru before the Spanish conquest

INDIGENOUS People who are the original inhabitants of an area

INSTITUTION A society, organisation or establishment which carries out governmental, scientific or educational work

INTENSIVE MODERN FARMING Growing in the smallest area and producing maximum yields using modern farming methods

INTERNET Global computer information network

INUIT A people who are originally from the Arctic

KRILL Tiny shrimplike creatures eaten by whales

LAND RECLAMATION Previously unusable land, sea or lake bed developed for agriculture etc

LEAD A heavy metal used for thousands of years for pipes, roofs, gutters etc.

MALARIA A dangerous disease transmitted by the bite of a certain type of mosquito

MANATEE A large aquatic plant-eating mammal with a large rounded body, short head and square muzzle

MANICOLE Large rat that lives in coconut palms

MARITIME CANADA The eastern provinces of Canada

MENINGITIS A serious disease that affects the brain and spinal cord

continued on next page

MERCURY   A very toxic heavy metal unique because it is liquid at room temperature

MICROBE   A very small organism eg algae, bacteria

MUNICIPAL   (Of) local government

MULTILATERAL   In which three or more parties take part

NATURAL FOOD PRODUCTS   Food which includes no artificial additives.

NGO   Non-governmental organisation

OZONE   A form of oxygen with three atoms in a molecule; found as a layer in the upper atmosphere, and close to the ground

PESTICIDE   Substance for destroying insects or other pests

PLANKTON   Microscopic life-forms found in oceans

POPs   Persistent Organic Pollutants – chemicals that pollute the environment and are especially harmful as they stay around for a long time

POVERTY   Living on less than one US dollar per day.

PROTOCOL   An amendment or addition to a treaty or convention

SANITATION   Pipes and treatment plants that drain sewage and refuse from houses

SALINITY   (Amount of) salt in water or soil

SEWAGE   Liquid waste and human faeces

SHANTY TOWN   Unplanned urban slum village where very poor people live. Usually found on the edge of big cities

SKIN CANCER   Cancer of the skin caused by over-exposure to sunlight

SMOKESTACK INDUSTRY An old-type industry identified by tall smoking chimneys

SOCIAL INDICATORS   Indicators of the well-being, educational status etc. of a society

SOIL EROSION   The process of wearing away soil by wind, rain, over-cultivation etc.

SOLAR ENERGY   Energy from the sun

SOLID WASTE   Garbage - domestic and industrial non-degradable waste materials

SPECIES   A certain type of plant or animal

SQUALOR   State of extreme poverty

STOCK MARKET   The system of buying and selling stocks and shares in public companies

SUBSIDIES   Money given by governments to keep down prices of vital goods and services

SUSTAINABLE DEVELOPMENT   Meeting the needs of today while ensuring that the future generation can meet their needs

TEMPERATE FOREST   Forests situated between the Tropic of Cancer and the Arctic Circle in the Northern Hemisphere or between the Tropic of Capricorn and the Antarctic Circle in the Southern Hemisphere. A climate which is warm in the summer, cold in the winter, and moderate in the spring and fall

TRADITIONAL FARMING   Way of farming that has been going on for generations

TROPICAL   Something inside the tropics

TROPICS   Regions between the Tropics of Cancer and Capricorn, latitudes 30° North and South of the equator

TUBERCULOSIS   Infectious disease of the lungs

TYPHOID (FEVER) Infectious fever causing rash and severe stomach problems & often death

UNEP   United Nations Environment Programme

URBANISATION   The building and growth of towns in rural areas

UV RAYS   Ultraviolet rays: an invisible form of energy harmful to most living organisms

VEGETATION   Plant life

WATER TABLE   The level of water in the Earth

WWF   World Wide Fund for Nature

Glossary

index

ECOmind maze!

Do you want to know how much you have learnt and remembered from our book? Our Mexican friends have created this maze which, like our planet, only those with environmental knowledge can navigate successfully!

What you Need

You will need: a dice and some stones or other natural objects as pieces to move around the board. (We copied the animal drawings and stuck them on the stones and sticks which looked great!) You will also need some paper or card: cut it into squares and circles then write all the questions on them. The answers to the questions can be found in the book. *You can read the questions straight off the book, but it is more fun to have them on paper beside the board.*

Starting the game

First elect a supreme ruler. This can be the teacher, but it can also be one of the students. The important thing is that the supreme ruler be elected by all the players. He/she will be coordinating the game and will be in charge of asking questions to the teams. If there is a dispute, the supreme ruler will decide it.

Fold out the game card on the back cover of the book; you find the rules on there as well; divide the question cards depending on the issue, shuffle each 'pack' and put them face down.

- Divide into teams of 3 or 4.
- Each team throws the dice. The team that throws the highest score starts, followed by the one that got the second highest and so on.
- The maximum number of teams that can play is 5.
- Place each team's game piece on the white rectangle on the board.

General & Atmosphere

Name all 7 environmental issues defined by GEO.

What could we tax to raise money to spend on saving the environment and ensure that only those who could afford it pay it?

What % of energy resources are used by the richest 20% of the world's population?

What does UNEP stand for?

What was the voluntary agreement reached at the Rio Earth Summit called?

What are the 'root causes' of environmental destruction'?

What are young people supposed to do as a result of reading this book?

What are the 3 forces driving environmental change?

What does Pachamama mean?

What does sustainable development mean?

Give 2 consequences of the hole in the ozone layer.

Give 3 common daily activities that pollute the air.

What does Aimee Robson mean by Mad Car Disease?

What do some people wear in cities to protect them from smog?

How many people died at Bhopal and why?

What causes global warming?

What are CFCs and what part of the atmosphere do they harm?

Name 4 diseases caused by air pollution.

Identify 5 ways that the person in the "Not my Fault" story contributes to global warming.

How does Cecilia Farfan describe her feelings living in the world's biggest city?

Freshwater & Forests

What is the main fear concerning freshwater according to GEO?

What are aquifers and water overdrafts?

Which 3 regions of the world are the most affected by water overdrafts?

How many children die every year from polluted water?

Name two regions that suffer severe flood problems.

Name 4 causes of water pollution.

What do we learn is a major reason for water shortages?

Name 3 things that make the Ganges river so sick.

Name 3 things that happened in Kenya as a result of the floods.

Why did the floods happen in Peru and why were they so damaging?

List 2 reasons why forests are so important.

Name 3 reasons why we destroy the rainforest.

Where are the largest rainforests in the world? How do forest fires affect the atmosphere?

3.7 million hectares of rainforest is lost every year – how many football pitches is that per hour?

Name 3 ways you can make money out of tearing down forests.

How long has Europe been without its original forests?

Why do you see miles and miles of dead trees in Central and East European forests?

Which are disappearing faster, temperate forests or rainforests, and why?

What are the chipkos? And what does chipko mean?

Biodiversity

What is an exotic species? Give a North American example.

What effects does introduction of exotic species have on biodiversity?

Name a major threat to the biodiversity of lakes and rivers in eastern and southern Africa.

What wiped out Dodos on Mauritius?

What was the aim of the Convention on Biological Diversity and who refused to sign it?

Why is Dolly so famous?

What is the main threat of genetic manipulation?

How many diverse species are there in the world? Do we know this for certain?

How many insect species were found in one tree in the Amazon rainforest?

Coasts & Polar regions

Name 3 things we do that destroy our coastal environment.

What are 2 environmental problems with fish farming?

What spreads like a horror movie and how does it happen?

How can algae tides be prevented?

What happens when more people move to the coasts?

What happens if coral reefs die?

Why are mangrove swamps important?

Why are fish catches globally falling now?

What is dynamite fishing?

Think of 6 ways that lives of sea turtles could be improved.

What are the Polar Regions?

How big is Antarctica?

Who are the Inuit?

What activities make up the economy of the Inuit?

Which two countries are exerting pressure to allow resumption of whale hunting?

What feeds on krill and plankton?

Name 2 things dumped in Murmansk harbour.

If global warming melted the polar icecaps, how much would sea level rise?

How many blue whales are left in the world now?

Why did Renée's father build an otter clinic?

Urbanisation

What % of the world's population now live in cities?

Name 3 horrors that come with massive urbanisation.

How much does the world's population grow every day?

Why would you wish to own a gas mask in Mexico City?

Name five ways you could reduce garbage [Zambia]?

What are shanty towns and why are they a problem?

In Guaiba, Brazil, what percentage of waste would be thrown away if it was properly sorted?

Apart from pollution, give another issue resulting from traffic which affects human beings.

How many people are estimated to be homeless in both developed and developing countries?

What is the most valuable resource for cities?

Land and Food

Name a major land-use problem faced by a third of the world's land.

What is desertification and how many people does it affect?

Why is urbanisation a problem?

How many people on average live on 1km^2 in Asia?

What is food security and how many countries will it affect by the year 2000?

What are POPs?

Name 2 solutions found in Australia to land degradation.

Why do Australian farmers hate salt?

How many trees were planted in Hajara's region?

The Future

What is the difference between an MEA and a Convention?

What 3 things ensured early compliance by countries to the Montreal Protocol?

What is an emerging issue?

What is ocean flip-flop?

Name 5 emerging issues identified by scientists?

What are green taxes?

Name 3 gaps in Agenda 21 identified by young people.

What is intelligent pricing? Do governments do it?

What is the difference between a binding and a non-binding agreement?

What does GEO suggest would be a visionary thing to do when it comes to governmental departments?

What does GEO suggest visionary leaders could do about water resources?

What you can do!

What is Green Fire and the YAC?

Why does Kruti Parekh promote worms?

What are EYA and YES? And what do they do?

What was the top positive youth emerging trend?

Name 2 things the Green Beans do with the money they raise.

What did the students of the Apeejay school do, in which city and why?

What do the Eco-teens of Indonesia do?

What is "Paradise in the city" and why?

How can you cook for the rest of your life for free?

Why did kids collect 4,800 pieces of plastic in Bhutan?

What is Planet Xpress?

Why do Kenyan Youth plant trees?

What have you ever done to save the world? (If nothing, go back three spaces!)

What should leaders do to protect forests, according to GEO?

What does John le Carré identify as the most important emerging issue?

What does David Bellamy believe is coming that makes him optimistic?

Circular questions

You find an injured sheep, chicken, monkey or rabbit in the road. What do you do?

You find that in the office, school or college you work in, there are no facilities for recycling, everyone drives to work and eats beef hamburgers for lunch. What do you do?

A salesman offers you a pack of genetically engineered seeds to grow in your garden. What do you do?

A scientist offers to clone you. What do you do?

You find a leaky tap in a public toilet. What do you do?

While taking an evening stroll in your local park with a friend, you find banana peels, beer and coke cans all over the place. What do you do?

Your father asks you to join him in cutting a tree from the nearby forest. What do you do?

Your sporty uncle drops in one day and invites you to go hunting during your holidays. What do you do?

While out camping in a scenic valley, your father asks you to join him in catching fish for lunch from a river. What do you do?

Some friends of yours encourage you to become a vegetarian or vegan. What do you do?

The small stream near your house is clogged and polluted with rubbish and silt and is turning into a breeding place for mosquitoes. What do you do?

Visiting a friend's office, you find that most of the waste — bins are filled with papers used on one side only. What do you do?

At your local food store or supermarket, a special promotion encourages you to buy food from organic farms. It is more expensive, so what do you do?

You hear that your government is planning to build a nuclear power station in your country. What do you do?

We are told that the population explosion is the greatest problem facing humanity. Do you agree? If so, is there anything that young people can, or should, do about it?

What other ways can you think of to keep food cool and preserved other than putting them in an electric fridge?

Unemployment is a great problem in many parts of the world, particularly for young people. Name three good things that young people can do to combat this problem.

Why do people in the North consume so much? Could they be persuaded to consume less?

When women have education and human rights, why is this better for the environment?

Why should youths be concerned about emerging issues?

Give three ideas on how to help people break off their love affairs with their cars.

Will you buy a car if it runs on petrol?

How does religion influence sustainable development?

Is there any hope for the Earth?

What alternatives do we have to consumerism?

If the developing countries became developed would that be good for the Earth? Why?

Why should all future development be sustainable?

Do you think democracies can save the Earth?

What kind of education would teach us all personal responsibility for the Earth?

What is the meaning of life?